SUCCESS SKILLS FOR MIDDLE SCHOOLERS:

How to Build Resilience, Confidence and Take Care of You

The Essential Middle School Survival Guide

FERNE BOWE

SOMETHING
FOR YOU

Get your **FREE** printable copy of the
"Life Skills for Tweens Workbook"

WITH OVER 80 FUN ACTIVITIES **JUST FOR TWEENS!**

**Scan the code to
download your
FREE printable copy**

TABLE OF CONTENTS

CHAPTER 1:

INTRODUCTION:
WHY MIDDLE SCHOOL MATTERS

Welcome to middle school!

You've worked hard to get here and should be proud of yourself for achieving this incredible milestone!

Middle school is an exciting time, full of new experiences and opportunities. You'll find yourself in a new school, where you will make new friends, take new classes, learn from new teachers, and participate in exciting new activities.

Everything about the experience of becoming a middle schooler can feel new and exciting. There is so much to explore and learn, but once the initial excitement fades, finding yourself in this wonderful new world can be challenging. Keeping up with homework, navigating new friendship groups, and changes in your body and emotions can make this time feel a little uncertain. Sometimes, life as a middle school student can feel like a whirlwind.

But here's a secret! What if I told you that everyone feels that way and that success in middle school isn't about having it all figured out? Instead, it's about learning some essential skills and strategies to help you survive in middle school and set you up for success.

That's where this book comes in. This book is designed to help you better understand the new world you now find yourself in and equip you with essential skills that can make all the difference in middle school and beyond.

Before we begin, let's first examine why middle school is so important.

Middle school is the intersection between elementary and high school and the transition between childhood and becoming a teenager. In other words, you're now officially a "tween."

In the past, your parents likely oversaw and organized your life, from supervising your homework to managing time with your friends.

But now that you're a middle schooler, these responsibilities will shift toward you. While your parents will continue to play significant roles, you'll gradually take on more responsibility. You'll become responsible for completing and submitting your homework assignments on time, choosing after-school activities, and organizing get-togethers with friends.

As a middle schooler, you'll also face new challenges, like homework assignments, navigating friendship groups, and eventually thinking about life after school and the steps you need to take to achieve your goals.

But don't worry—you're not alone on this journey. In fact, developing the skills in this book will help you tackle all of these challenges more confidently.

Before we get to that, what are success skills?

Success skills are practical skills that will help you achieve your goals and navigate the challenges and opportunities of everyday life. These include time management, social skills, study habits, communication skills, self-care, and many more. They are essential for success in school and can help you lead a happy, successful, fulfilling life.

Think of success skills as the tools in your toolbox that can help you build the life you want. Just as a carpenter needs the right tools to build a house, you need the right tools to succeed in life. And just like the carpenter, who learns how to saw wood or hammer nails by practicing, you can develop your success skills through practice and hard work.

Middle school is the ideal time to develop these skills. As your responsibilities increase during high school and beyond, having strong success skills will help you navigate new situations with ease, deal with problems effectively, and take advantage of opportunities that come your way.

This book will cover all the essential success skills you need, including:

- Time management
- Staying organized and on top of schoolwork
- Effective communication
- Developing a growth mindset
- Embracing challenges as opportunities for growth

- Understanding emotions
- Looking after yourself
- Setting goals and reaching them
- Preparing for high school and beyond

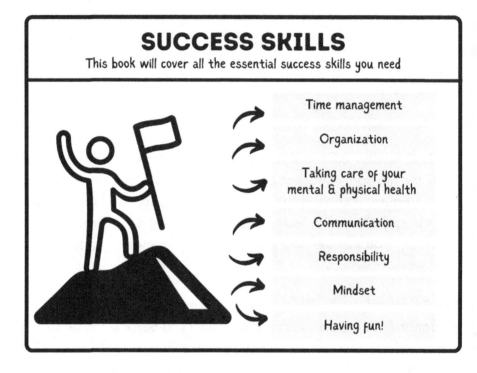

Equipped with the success skills you'll learn in this book, you will be able to confidently tackle middle school and any adventures that lie ahead.

Let's get started!

CHAPTER 2:

TIME MANAGEMENT

Time is fleeting.
Time and tide wait for no one.
Time is the most valuable thing a person can spend.
Time is what we want most, but what we use worst.
Time is a precious gift. Use it wisely.

You've probably heard some of these quotes about time and how people use it.

Time is the one thing we can't control, and you can never get it back when it's gone. However, once you've mastered the skill of time management, you'll be better at using your time wisely.

. . . .
SECTION 1: UNDERSTANDING TIME MANAGEMENT

Time is always ticking away.

It often slips away if we don't find ways to manage it.

But what exactly is time management, and how do time management skills help us?

Time management is the skill of planning and organizing your time efficiently to accomplish your goals.

In other words, mastering time management gives you the tools to effectively manage time and use it to your advantage!

As a middle schooler, time management can be a significant challenge. School work, after-school activities, meeting friends, family time, TV, and video games compete for your attention. There is never enough time to do everything.

But you'll feel more in control once you learn to manage your time effectively. In fact, having a practical plan for allocating your time can help you reduce stress, get more done, and set you on a path to success in your school and personal life.

Time management strategies we will cover in this chapter include:

● Creating a daily schedule
● Prioritizing tasks
● Avoiding distractions and maintaining focus
● Putting time management skills into practice in everyday life

Before any more time slips away, let's get started!

SECTION 2: HOW TO CREATE A DAILY SCHEDULE

Creating a daily schedule is one of the most effective ways to manage your time.

You may not realize it, but you have been following a schedule for some time now. You have set times for waking up and going to school. When you arrive at school, your classes and lunchtime are scheduled. You leave school and go home at a specific time. Once you get home, you probably have scheduled activities, such as dance or music lessons or family events. If you participate in sports at school, you're expected to be there at a set time.

These are schedules created by your parents or school to keep your life organized and on track.

But as a middle schooler, you are now ready to start creating your own schedule!

Creating a daily schedule will help you plan and use your time best, making balancing your homework, school projects, activities, and time with your friends easier. Here's how to create your schedule in five easy steps:

Step I: Identify your peak productivity time.

Before creating your daily schedule, it's important to identify your peak productivity time.

What is peak productivity time?

Peak productivity time is when you are most productive. It's the time of day when your concentration and energy levels are highest, which means you can do the most important tasks!

Everyone is unique. Some people work best in the morning, while others find focusing easier later in the day.

The key is to identify when you feel most productive. It could be before school, during your lunch break, after school, or on the weekend.

Once you determine your peak productivity time, use it to schedule the tasks that require total focus. This could include doing homework, practicing an instrument, or learning lines for a school play. Whatever it is, use this time wisely.

Step 2: Keep track of your daily activities.

Keep track of the activities you do every day in a notepad or calendar. These include: when you wake up, travel to school, after-school activities, when you do your homework, and anything else you do regularly. Noting these down for a week or two will help determine how long each activity takes. It may also highlight areas where you can be more productive!

Step 3: Use a planner to add in your activities.

Use a planner or notepad to record your daily schedule beginning with your routine activities. *For example, "7:00–8:30 morning routine."*

When you start, try different types of planners to find the one that works best for you. You may prefer using a paper planner, but there are also many excellent calendar apps that you can use on digital devices.

If you prefer using a paper notebook, allow enough space for each day's activities and include the day of the week at the top of each page.

Step 4: Include regular breaks in your schedule.

It's impossible to perform at your best without taking breaks. Studying continuously for hours is usually unproductive and can lead to burnout. That's why it's essential to add breaks to your schedule.

Here are some tips to help you include breaks in your schedule:

- **Study time:** Determine how long you can study before needing a break. For most tweens, it's around 20 to 40 minutes.

- **Time it:** Set a timer for that period, then get to work on your assignments.

- **Take a break:** When the timer goes off, take a break. Go for a walk, dance to your favorite music, or do something relaxing and fun. Try to do something that is completely disconnected from your work.

- **Get back to work:** After your break, return to work feeling refreshed and ready to learn!

Here's an example of a simple daily schedule for a middle schooler:

DAILY SCHEDULE

TIME	ACTIVITIES LIST
7:30-8:30	Morning routine (getting ready for school)
8:30-9:00	Travel to school
9:00-3:00	School (follow the school schedule for classes and lunch)
3:00-4:00	After-school football practice
4:00-4:45	Travel home and snack break
4:45-5:15	Homework or project work (peak productivity time)
5:15-5:30	Break (15-30 minutes to relax and recharge)
5:30-6:00	Continue homework or project work
6:00-7:00	Dinner and family time
7:00-8:00	Free time (spend time with friends, watch TV, or play video games)
8:00-8:30	Evening routine (prepare for the next day and get ready for bed)

Remember to be flexible with your schedule. As your priorities and the activities you are involved with change, so will your schedule. Just ensure you have enough time to relax, have fun, and recharge your batteries with friends and family.

. . . .

SECTION 3: HOW TO PRIORITIZE TASKS

Effectively prioritizing tasks is essential to time management. You can make the most of your time by first identifying and doing the most important, urgent, and highest-priority tasks.

Identifying high-priority tasks is straightforward.

1. **Create a task list:** Write down all the tasks you must complete and include a due date.

2. **Use the ABC Method:** Prioritize tasks based on their importance using The ABC Method. Assign the most critical tasks a letter "A," less essential tasks a "B," and non-essential tasks (or things that are nice to do but that you can technically go without) a letter "C." Finally, number them in order of importance.

3. **Schedule high-priority tasks first:** High-priority activities should be added to your schedule first and done during your most productive hours to ensure they're completed on time and to the best of your ability.

   For example, a school project due soon would be regarded as high priority (A), while going to a mall with friends can wait until later, so it would be assigned a lower priority (C).

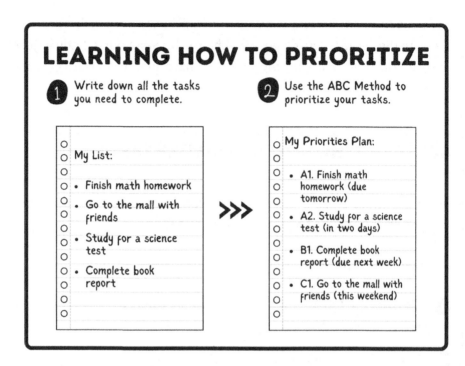

LEARNING HOW TO PRIORITIZE

1 Write down all the tasks you need to complete.

2 Use the ABC Method to prioritize your tasks.

My List:

• Finish math homework

• Go to the mall with friends

• Study for a science test

• Complete book report

>>>

My Priorities Plan:

• A1. Finish math homework (due tomorrow)

• A2. Study for a science test (in two days)

• B1. Complete book report (due next week)

• C1. Go to the mall with friends (this weekend)

Of course, making the most of your time and prioritizing effectively also requires you to sometimes say no and cut out some time-wasting activities. Let's look at both of these:

How to Reduce Time-Wasting Activities

One way to make more time for things you want to do is by cutting out or reducing time-wasting activities, like checking social media, browsing the Internet, or binge-watching TV shows.

These activities can be enjoyed in moderation but spending too much time on them may be unproductive and get in the way of completing important tasks. Here's what you should do:

1 **Create a plan:** Decide when and for how long you'll do these activities each day. Set specific times and daily limits for yourself.

For example: "I will only check social media for a maximum of 30 minutes a day."

2 **Schedule time:** Create time in your daily schedule for these activities.

3 **Stick to your schedule:** Stick to your daily or weekly program.

How to Say "No"

Sometimes, people ask you to do things you aren't interested in. *For example, a friend might ask you to go see a movie you don't think you'll enjoy, or someone might ask for help with a project when you are already short on time.* Whatever the situation, it's important to remember that you always have the right to say "no."

HOW TO SAY "NO"

Here are some tips on how to say "no" politely and effectively:

1 **BE POLITE & CONFIDENT**
Be polite and confident when declining an invitation.

2 **SUGGEST AN ALTERNATIVE**
Suggest an alternative activity or time that is more in sync with your interests and preferences.

3 **KEEP PRACTICING**
Practice makes perfect. The more you become comfortable with saying "no" the easier it will become.

Don't feel bad about saying "no." By declining invitations, you are protecting your time and making it available for things that matter to you. Saying "no" to someone often feels uncomfortable, but it doesn't mean you're being unkind or selfish. Instead, it shows others that you respect your own needs and are careful about how you spend your time.

Here are some tips on how to say "no" politely and effectively:

1. **Be polite:** Always be polite when declining an invitation. Offer a brief explanation as to why you have to decline the invitation, if appropriate. *For example, you might say, "Thanks for inviting me, I would have loved to come, but I already have other family plans."*

2. **Be confident:** Sometimes, you may feel guilty about letting a friend down. But once you decide, be confident and firm with your answer.

3. **Give them an alternative:** Suggest an alternative activity or time that may be better for you.

4. **Keep practicing:** Practice makes perfect. The more comfortable you are with saying "no," the easier it will become.

Learning to say no can be challenging, but once you practice and feel comfortable with it, you can ensure you do what is best for you.

. . . .

SECTION 4: HOW TO STAY FOCUSED AND AVOID DISTRACTIONS

Distractions, like social media and technology, can make it difficult to concentrate and complete essential tasks. If you're not careful, text messages, notifications, and app alerts can break your concentration, making it tough to focus and get homework or other important work done.

Here are a couple of simple ways to help you stay focused and avoid these types of digital distractions:

1. **Set devices to silent:** Set devices to silent until you have finished your homework or other important tasks. Remember, all those messages and notifications will still be there, waiting for you when you're ready to read them!

2. **Manage notifications:** If you're using a computer for your work, turn off notifications to reduce distractions.

How to Avoid Putting Things Off

Have you ever put off starting an assignment? Instead of starting the project, perhaps you found another more "important" task to tackle, like tidying your room or rearranging your books? That's procrastination!

Procrastination is when you delay or postpone an important task and choose to do something easier but usually less critical instead.

Procrastination is very common—in fact, everyone procrastinates occasionally. It usually happens when you feel stressed, overwhelmed, or unsure how to begin something.

Although putting off starting that important project might seem like a good temporary solution, it can cause more stress and take away time from the fun activities you could enjoy once that project is finished.

Here are some tips to help you avoid putting things off:

1 **Ask yourself why:** Identify the reason, and work backward. *For example, if you are putting off a project because you need clarification about the topic, speak to your teacher.*

2 **Break it down:** Break down larger projects into smaller, more manageable parts that you can tick off.

3 **Prioritize:** Prioritize tasks using the ABC Method and add them to your to-do list.

4 **Get started:** Once you have a clear idea of what you must do, the best way to get it done is to begin.

5 **Use The Pomodoro technique:** Focus on a task for 25 minutes, then take a five-minute break.

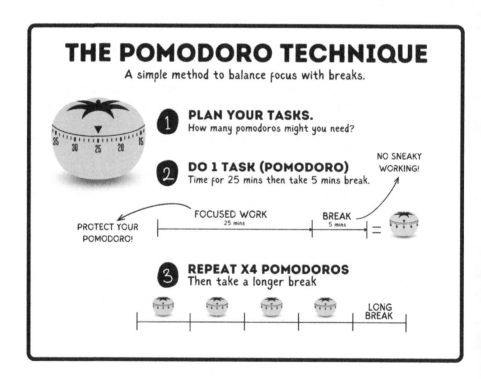

6 **Reward yourself:** Reward yourself after completing a task, however small.

Both methods help streamline your work and maintain momentum, making completing tasks easier and more effective.

Nobody's Perfect: Avoid the Perfectionist Trap

When you start learning time management, remember that it's a new experience. There may be times when you forget to write something down or include a task in your schedule. If this happens, don't be too hard on yourself. Nobody is perfect, and your time management skills will improve with practice!

Stay positive, keep learning, and make changes as you go. You'll be a time management superstar in no time!

• •

SECTION 5: PUTTING IT INTO PRACTICE

Now that you're familiar with time management, it's time to implement these valuable skills!

Here's a to-do list to help you get started:

1 **Identify your peak productivity times:** Allocate this time for the most important tasks.

2 **Track your activities:** Keep track of your daily activities and add them to a planner.

3 **Prioritize:** Compile a list of all your tasks and include their due date. Prioritize them using the ABC method.

④ Include regular breaks: Try using the Pomodoro Technique and work in 25-minute bursts, followed by a five-minute break.

⑤ Say "no": Don't feel bad about saying "no" to activities that don't align with your goals and priorities.

⑥ Get started: Turn off devices to avoid being distracted, and get started.

Remember, practice makes perfect, and you'll become better at managing your time as you continue to implement these strategies.

Why not try using the weekly planner on the next page. Good luck!

WEEKLY PLANNER

Weekly priorities

_____
_____
_____
_____
_____

Notes

Monday	Tuesday	Wednesday	Thursday	Friday	Saturday	Sunday

Checklist

☐ _____
☐ _____
☐ _____
☐ _____
☐ _____
☐ _____
☐ _____
☐ _____
☐ _____
☐ _____
☐ _____

Appointment

_____

Reminder

_____

CHAPTER 3:

STAYING ORGANIZED

"For every minute spent in organizing, an hour is earned."
— Benjamin Franklin, Founding Father.

As a middle school student, you'll lead a busy life with many exciting activities. In addition to school and homework, your days will be filled with meeting friends, after-school activities, and family events. With so much happening, keeping up with everything can be challenging and sometimes stressful!

With your busy schedule packed full of activities, the last thing on your mind might be getting organized.

However, learning to organize your life is one of the most crucial skills you can develop. An organized student always knows what they need to do and where they can find the supplies they need for the task. The organizational skills you develop now can help you succeed in middle school, high school, college, and beyond.

In this chapter, we'll look at the advantages of being organized and provide strategies for effectively managing schoolwork and after-school activities. In addition, we'll cover some valuable tips for keeping your physical and digital spaces tidy.

Topics we'll cover in this chapter include:

- The benefits of being organized
- Staying on top of schoolwork
- Managing after-school activities
- Keeping your physical and digital spaces tidy

Once you master these skills, you'll see firsthand the positive impact staying organized can have on your life!

. . . .

SECTION 1: THE BENEFITS OF BEING ORGANIZED

When you are organized, you're a student with a plan for success! You know what you need to do and when you need to do it. You also know what supplies you need for a project and where to find them. Because of this, you feel confident about your ability to get things done.

❶ You'll be more productive.

Being organized and being more productive are closely connected. The more organized you are, the more effective you can be.

So, what exactly does it mean to be productive?

Being productive is about using your time. energy. and resources in a way that helps you achieve your goals and get things done efficiently and effectively.

Being organized is the key to productivity. When you're organized, you don't waste time figuring out what to do next or searching for things you need to complete a project. Instead, you use your time and energy to focus on the task.

For example, imagine you have an art project due next week, and you know it will require some research, creativity, and specific materials. Instead of leaving it to the last minute, you plan ahead.

1. You break the project down into small tasks.

2. You spend a day researching the project.

3. You list the materials you'll need and gather them over the weekend.

Now that everything is in place, you work on the project step-by-step during the week, using a schedule to track your progress. By the time the project is due, you've completed it successfully without any last-minute stress.

② Your thinking will be clearer and more organized.

As you apply organizing skills, you will notice that your thinking gradually becomes clearer and more organized. This is a natural outcome of worrying less about forgetting things or missing deadlines.

Clear and organized thinking leads to the following:

- **Better focus:** Since you aren't distracted by random thoughts or worries, you can concentrate on the task and complete projects more efficiently.

- **Improved memory:** You'll find learning and remembering information more straightforward, which will help you do better in school.

- **Better decision-making:** You'll be able to make smarter choices about using your time in ways that align with your goals.

- **Reduced stress:** When you clearly understand what you need to do and when you need to do it, you'll feel calmer and more in control.

- **Boosted creativity:** You'll be able to think more creatively. Freed from disorganized thoughts and worries, you'll find it easier to generate innovative new ideas.

In short, clear and organized thinking will help you be more successful in school and life!

③ You'll feel less stressed.

Many middle school students report struggling with stress, anxiety, and feeling overwhelmed due to increased homework, after-school activities, and other commitments. But being organized can help reduce these feelings, as it puts you in control of your life, makes you more productive, and enables you to make the best use of your time.

SECTION 2: HOW TO STAY ON TOP OF SCHOOLWORK

Staying on top of schoolwork is a significant challenge for many students. With so much happening, it's easy to forget assignments or put them off until the night before they are due. That's why staying organized and having a detailed plan to help you stay on track is so important.

Tips for Managing Assignments, Projects, and Deadlines

Keeping up with school assignments is vital for making good grades. Here are some tips to help you become an organizational superstar!

MAKE USE OF
PLANNING TOOLS

PAPER PLANNERS

- Bullet Journal
- Daily Schedule Planner
- Academic Planner
- Financial Planner
- To Do Lists

DIGITAL PLANNERS

- Evernote
- OneNote
- Trello
- Google Calendar
- Asana

- **Use a planner:** Keep track of school assignments, projects, and deadlines. Decide between a paper planner or a digital planner accessible on a phone, computer, or other device. Write down all the important dates and information for each class and check it regularly to ensure you're on track and not falling behind on any of your assignments.

- **Start a calendar:** Mark down all of your commitments and activities. In addition to keeping track of school assignments, use your calendar to note family events, plans with your friends, concerts, sports games, and other activities you want to do. Sharing this calendar with your parents and other family members will make it less likely for them to schedule a family event when you have something else planned.

- **Create a daily to-do list:** Make a list of daily tasks to stay on track with everything happening in your life. Remember to prioritize high-importance tasks, such as completing homework assignments and studying for upcoming tests.

- **Use electronic reminders:** Even when using a planner effectively, it's easy to lose track of time when working on a project or activity. Set the alarm on your phone or computer to notify you that it's time to take a break or move on to another item on your to-do list. Knowing you'll hear the "ding" of the alarm when it's time to move on to the next task can help you stay focused on the task at hand.

How to Tackle Big Projects

Sometimes, a teacher may give you a big project that initially seems overwhelming. You know you must do it to get a good grade, but you don't see how you'll finish it on time. Just thinking about all the work involved can be stressful.

Don't worry! Once you learn to break down large projects into smaller tasks, you won't feel like you're running a marathon without doing the training. Instead, you'll feel confident that you can do a bunch of shorter races that you're well prepared for.

Here are some steps that will help you complete any big project:

1 **Understand the assignment first.** Carefully read the project to ensure you understand what is expected. Try to see the big picture and get a good understanding of what needs to be done. If you have questions about the assignment, now's the time to ask your teacher.

2 **Break the project down.** Identify and list the key steps to complete the project. *For example, if your teacher asks you to write a research paper on the history of space exploration since the early 1960s, your first step would be to research the space program. You could then break that down into smaller parts.*

By breaking the task down, you can focus on one task at a time, making the project much more manageable.

3 **Make an outline.** Create an outline to organize your thoughts.

4 **Estimate the time.** Try to work out how long each task will take. It takes time to perfectly estimate the time needed for tasks, so it's better to give yourself more time when you start.

5 **Plan your time.** Schedule time for each task and note it in your planner. Prioritize more significant tasks requiring more time and effort to ensure you progress on the most critical tasks first.

6 **Allow extra time.** Block out additional time on your schedule for large projects in case you run into problems. This will reduce any stress about hitting your deadline.

7 **Review your planner.** Make sure you've included everything and that you haven't missed anything.

8 **Check your planner.** Regularly check your planner to stay on track and avoid falling behind. Your planner is your best tool for managing your large project and minimizing stress as you complete it.

Watch Out for Rabbit Holes!

A rabbit hole isn't just a place where rabbits live. In today's language, "going down a rabbit hole" means getting lost in a topic and forgetting the reason or goal of the task.

> *For example, let's say your music class studies 1980s rock music, and your teacher asks you to look up some simple facts about '80s rock bands.*
>
> *But after searching "1980s rock," you spend hours watching music videos, learning about different types of '80s music, and listening to various bands. You have "gone down the rabbit hole" of 1980s rock music!*

Going down rabbit holes isn't a bad thing. In fact, it often leads to discovering interesting information. It can be an essential part of learning about a new topic. However, it's crucial to maintain a balance between exploration and focusing on the end goal.

To achieve this balance, consider setting specific goals and time limits for your research. For instance, in the example above, by allocating a certain amount of time for researching different bands, you can still enjoy exploring new music while ensuring you stay on schedule to complete the project.

SECTION 3: HOW TO MANAGE AFTER-SCHOOL ACTIVITIES

As a middle schooler, you will likely be involved in various after-school activities, like sports, choir, chess, or drama club. Although they're not part of your regular classes, these activities are a valuable and fun part of your school experience.

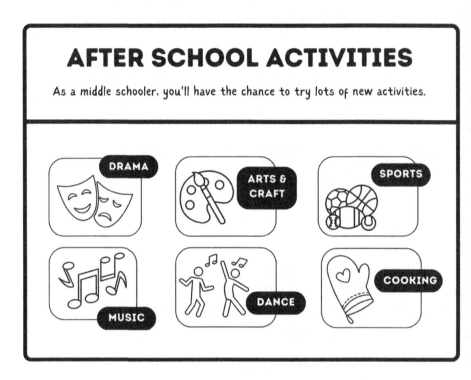

AFTER SCHOOL ACTIVITIES

As a middle schooler, you'll have the chance to try lots of new activities.

Participating in after-school activities offers many benefits, including:

- Meeting other students with similar interests.
- A feeling of belonging and purpose.
- Boosting your self-confidence, social skills, communication skills, and teamwork abilities.
- A chance to develop new talents and improve existing skills outside the classroom.
- A chance to stand out when applying for college, as your interests and activities can highlight your unique abilities.

TIPS FOR JUGGLING SCHOOLWORK AND ACTIVITIES

PUT SCHOOLWORK FIRST:

Schedule essential homework assignments and other school projects that affect your grades ahead of your other activities.

CHECK YOUR COMMITMENTS:

Review your list of activities and responsibilities, such as babysitting, pet sitting, or daily chores, to ensure that any extracurricular activities you sign up for don't interfere with your existing commitments.

DON'T OVERCOMMIT YOURSELF:

Be careful not to take on more than you can handle. While it's natural and great to explore new interests, you'll eventually want to focus on the activities that interest you most.

TALK TO YOUR FAMILY:

If your parents or other family members drive you to these activities, check their availability first.

USE YOUR PLANNER AND CALENDAR:

These tools help balance extracurricular activities with school and other plans. Mark down all the days and times you'll spend on extracurricular activities.

BE FLEXIBLE AND MAKE ADJUSTMENTS:

If you are overwhelmed by the number of activities you pursue, consider reducing your involvement to focus on the remaining activities without feeling stressed.

Remember that managing your time and staying organized takes practice. Be easy on yourself if you forget to write something in your planner. With persistence and consistent use of your planner, you will soon feel confident in your ability to manage everything going on in your life.

· ·

SECTION 4: HOW TO KEEP YOUR WORK SPACES TIDY

Being organized isn't just about schoolwork and activities; it's also about keeping your physical and digital spaces tidy. You can better focus on your tasks when these spaces are clean and tidy.

How to Organize Your Physical Space

Your backpack, study area at home, and locker are all part of your physical workspace. When these are messy or disorganized, it can make it difficult to focus. Keeping these spaces tidy will help increase your productivity and success in middle school.

Here are some tips for organizing your backpack, locker, and study area:

1. **Clean out your backpack once a week:** Take everything out, throw away trash you might have accumulated (like snack wrappers), and remove items you no longer need. This will make you less likely to misplace or forget important things like homework assignments, notebooks, and textbooks.

2. **Use your backpack's pockets:** If your bag has pockets, use them for different items. Keep small items like your keys, calculator, pens, and pencils in one pocket and your planner and homework in another.

3 **Get locker shelves or dividers:** If your school locker doesn't already have shelves or dividers, adding them yourself can help you stay organized. They make finding your books and other school supplies easier for each class. As with your backpack, remember to clean out your locker regularly.

4 **Keep your study area clean and clutter-free:**. A tidy workspace will help you focus better. Try to limit your workspace to essential items you need for studying.

5 **Organize small items in containers:** Use containers for small items, such as pens, pencils, and paper clips. This makes them easy to find when you need them.

How to Organize Your Digital Space

Organizing and tidying your digital space is as important as managing your physical space. Digital space includes your computer, tablet, or phone (if you have one). Here are some tips to help you get started:

1 **Group items together:** Create main folders on your computer for subjects, personal projects, and hobbies. This will help you quickly find and access the files you need.

2 **Use subfolders:** Within your main folders, create subfolders to better organize your files.

3 **Name files clearly:** Use descriptive file names. *For example, instead of naming a "homework.doc" file, use a descriptive title such as "2023-04-01 Math-Algebra-Homework.doc."* This clearly shows the date, the subject (math), the topic (algebra), and the type of assignment (homework).

4 **Be consistent:** Apply the same file naming system to all your files. This will help you stay organized and save time searching for specific information.

5 **Keep your desktop clean:** Only keep the apps and files you need for quick access on your desktop.

6 **Review and delete unwanted files (or apps):** Every month, set aside some time to remove unwanted files. This will help your computer stay clutter-free and will help it run faster.

How to Manage Your Email

1 **Set up filters:** Create rules in your email inbox to sort emails by sender, subject, or level of importance. This will help you pri-oritize and quickly locate essential emails.

2 **Unsubscribe:** Unsubscribe from unwanted email newsletters or promotions. Click the "unsubscribe" link within the email to remove yourself from their mailing list.

3 **Delete and archive emails:** This will help you stay orga-nized and avoid running out of digital storage space.

Remember, organizing your digital space requires ongoing maintenance. Schedule some time every week or month to clean and organize your digital spaces, just like you would with your physical space.

SECTION 5: PUTTING IT INTO PRACTICE

Being organized can help you be more productive and successful in school and in life. If you make staying organized a habit, it can improve your time management and focus while also reducing your stress. Stay as organized as possible, and you'll soon see that it makes a difference in your life!

Here are some suggestions for putting what you've read in this chapter into practice:

1. **Choose your planner:** Decide if you want to use a digital or paper organizer. Once you have what you need, start filling it in with your schoolwork and other commitments.

2. **List your priorities:** Make a list of priorities in your life, including school, extracurricular activities, recreational activities, time with friends, and family events.

3. **Keep your list handy:** List your priorities in front of your planner to check as you make your schedule.

4. **Break down large projects:** Break down larger projects into easily manageable tasks.

5. **Organize your spaces:** Set a time to organize your backpack, study area, locker, and digital spaces.

These strategies will help build strong organizational habits that will serve you well throughout school and beyond.

CHAPTER 4:

EFFECTIVE COMMUNICATION

"Communication is a skill that you can learn. It's like riding a bicycle or typing."
— Brian Tracy, self-development author and speaker.

Effective communication is an essential skill for middle school students. How you communicate significantly influences how others see you, whether in person, on social media, on the phone, via email, or in texts. Your communication skills play a crucial role in your relationships with friends, family, and other people you encounter.

Effective communication is crucial in getting a job, working with others to solve problems, and leading a happy and successful life outside school.

So, what exactly is communication?

Communication is exchanging information between people using a commonly understood system of language, symbols, signs, or behaviors.

In short, every interaction you have with others is a form of communication. *For example, when you buy a drink from a store, you communicate with the cashier. When you order a pizza delivery, you have to share your order.* In fact, even before you speak to someone, the way you sit and hold yourself is a form of nonverbal communication.

In this chapter, we'll explore the primary types of communication you'll use, including verbal, nonverbal, and written communication. Plus, we'll provide strategies to help you develop your communications skills and become a superstar communicator!

Topics covered in this chapter include:

● Understanding communication
● Effective listening
● Effective speaking and writing
● Understanding body language
● Resolving conflicts and building healthy relationships

Let's dive in!

· ·

SECTION 1: UNDERSTANDING COMMUNICATION

Before we start, let's look at the most common types of communication: verbal, nonverbal, and written. Here's a simple explanation of each type and how they are used.

TYPES OF COMMUNICATION

① VERBAL COMMUNICATION	② NONVERBAL COMMUNICATION	③ WRITTEN COMMUNICATION
Video calls, classroom discussions, presentations, phone calls, chatting with friends.	Body language, facial expressions, eye contact, hand gestures, posture, touch, personal space, clothing and appearance.	Emails, text messages, letters, reports, essays, social media posts, diaries, homework assignments.

- **Verbal communication:** This is when you use words to share a message, such as talking with friends, doing video calls, talking to your teacher, or giving a presentation.

- **Nonverbal communication:** This is when you share a message of emotions or feelings without using words. It includes facial expressions, body language, gestures, and tone of voice. Smiling, laughing, shrugging, and frowning are all examples of nonverbal communication.

- **Written communication:** This is when you use written words to share a message. This includes written homework, emails, texts, letters, books, magazines, and newspapers.

Developing good communication and listening skills is super important in middle school and beyond. These skills will help you ask intelligent questions, write clearly and effectively, understand body language, and express yourself.

SECTION 2: HOW TO LISTEN EFFECTIVELY

Being a good listener is an essential communication skill. If you learn to be a good listener while in middle school, this skill will help you throughout life. The better you become at listening, the easier it will be to understand and remember what people tell you.

How to Be A Good Listener

Have you ever shared an exciting story only to realize the listener wasn't listening to what you said? It can be annoying, but with so many things competing for our attention, it's easy to get distracted during a conversation. That's why it's essential to learn to be an active listener.

What is active listening?

Active listening is a way of listening and responding that encourages mutual respect and understanding. When you're actively listening, you're not just listening to the words someone says—you're also paying attention to their body language and emotions.

Learning and practicing active listening techniques is a great way to improve your communication skills. These skills can help you listen in a way that builds strong relationships and enables you to understand others better.

Here are some ways you can practice active listening:

1. **Pay attention:** Concentrate fully on the person speaking.

2. **Maintaining eye contact:** Maintaining eye contact shows the speaker that you are interested in what they are saying. It also helps you pick up non-verbal communication cues that can provide additional insights.

3. **Put your phone away:** Looking at your phone while someone is talking can be rude. Put it away and keep it on silent.

4. **Ask questions:** Asking questions shows you are interested and want to learn more. This can help you to gain a deeper understanding of what the person is trying to communicate.

5. **Don't interrupt:** Wait until the speaker has finished before asking questions or responding. Interrupting disrupts the flow of a conversation and shows that you're more interested in speaking than listening.

6. **Paraphrase:** If you're unsure what someone is saying, restate the message in your own words. "So, what you're saying is..." This technique is known as paraphrasing and ensures you have understood them correctly.

7. **Consider the emotions being expressed:** While listening, reflect on their emotions. Pay attention to their tone: Are they happy, sad, worried, or angry? Sometimes, people express their feelings in obvious ways, but other times, they are subtle and require close attention.

HOW TO BE AN ACTIVE LISTENER

Checklist

Keep eye contact.

Concentrate on the speaker.

Keep your phone on silent and out of sight.

Engage with the speaker by asking relevant questions.

Don't interrupt the speaker.

Restate the speaker's message in your own words.

Be aware of your own gestures and body language.

Jot down key points or keywords.

Be grateful and thank the speaker.

Try not to daydream!

If something is unclear. ask.

Tips for Asking Effective Questions

Asking questions is one of the best ways to ensure you understand what someone is saying.

Here are some tips on how to ask effective questions and seek clarification:

- **In class, take note of key points.** Wait until your teacher has finished speaking before asking any questions you might have.

- **Be respectful in your language and tone.** When you want more information, use polite language, such as, "Excuse me" or "May I ask a question?"

- **Ask open-ended questions.** Open-ended questions encourage the speaker to expand on their thoughts and ideas. *For example, "Can you tell me more about...?" or "What do you think about...?"*

- **Ask follow-up questions.** These questions can help you better understand the speaker's message. *For example, "How did you come to that conclusion?" or "Could you provide me with an example of what you mean?"*

- **If you're uncertain about something, don't be afraid to ask for clarification.** It's better to ask for more information than to come away with an assumption that might be wrong.

SECTION 3: HOW TO SPEAK AND WRITE EFFECTIVELY

Effective speaking and writing are two more skills you'll need to learn to become an effective communicator. These skills include speaking clearly and confidently and using the right tone of voice and body language to help get your message across.

Effective Speaking

Effective speaking is just as important as effective listening. Both of these skills are used daily in school, with friends, and in any clubs or groups you join.

Here are some tips to help you speak clearly and confidently:

- **Make eye contact.** Good eye contact is crucial for both listening and speaking. By looking at the other person, you show them that you wish to communicate even before you've said a word.

- **Speak at a steady pace.** If you talk too fast, it can be difficult for people to understand what you are saying, giving the impression that you're nervous.

- **Stand tall when you are speaking.** This shows that you are confident! If you're using notes for a report or presentation, hold them at a comfortable reading height so you don't need to bend over to read them.

- **Use the right tone.** Ensure that your tone matches the emotion you're trying to express.

- **Change your tone.** Good speakers use different tones for different parts of their messages. This helps them connect with their audiences and makes their talks more interesting.

- **Be aware of your facial expressions and body language.** These non-verbal forms of communication help emphasize a point you want to make and effectively convey your emotions.

- **Record videos of yourself talking.** Watching these videos may be awkward to begin with. Still, it will help you identify your strengths and weaknesses and give you an idea of how others see you.

Learning to speak clearly and confidently takes practice, so don't get discouraged. Be patient with yourself, and keep on practicing! If you keep working at it, you'll soon be a confident speaker!

Now, let's look at how you can excel at written communication.

Effective Writing

As a middle schooler, you'll have to complete written assignments. Learning how to better organize your writing will make finishing your homework on time easier. Plus, being good at written communication will help you later in life, such as when you apply for college, fill out job applications, or find yourself in any other situation that requires you to write your thoughts down on paper.

Here are some tips to help organize and improve your writing:

- **Think first:** Before you start writing, stop and think about what you want to say.

- **Create an outline:** Once you know what you'll be writing about, create an outline that includes your main points and the order in which you'll write them.

- **Use graphic organizers:** Graphic organizers, such as mind maps and flowcharts, are a great way to organize your ideas and create a structure for your writing. You can create graphic organizers on paper or use a program or app on your computer.

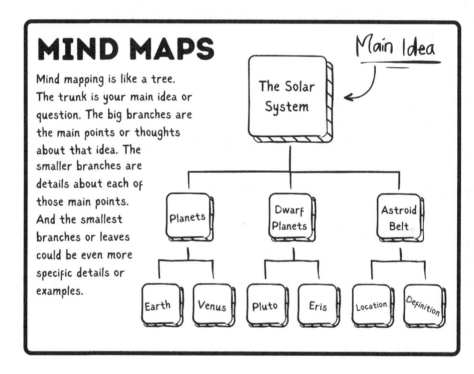

MIND MAPS

Mind mapping is like a tree. The trunk is your main idea or question. The big branches are the main points or thoughts about that idea. The smaller branches are details about each of those main points. And the smallest branches or leaves could be even more specific details or examples.

Main Idea

The Solar System

Planets

Dwarf Planets

Astroid Belt

Earth   Venus   Pluto   Eris   Location   Definition

- **Introduce topics:** Begin each paragraph with a sentence that introduces the reader to the main point of the section. *For example:* *"Reading isn't just for fun; it also helps you learn about new things."*

- **Add supporting information:** After the first sentence, add supporting information to strengthen your ideas and provide evidence for your arguments. Include specific examples, facts, and statistics to support your points. *For example: "When you read a science fiction book, you get to learn about different galaxies, creatures and people from different planets."*

- **Use transitional words:** Use transitional words and phrases like "because," "however," and "in addition" to provide strong links of connection between your ideas.

- **Check your work:** Once you've finished writing, check your work to ensure it is well-organized and has no spelling mistakes. Look for areas to improve, and make sure your writing flows smoothly from one idea to the next.

- **Get feedback:** When you are finished and believe you have done your best, ask a family member, teacher, or friend to read your writing and give you feedback.

As with any other skill, organizing and structuring your writing takes practice, so be patient with yourself. As you work on these skills, you'll soon see improvements!

Changing How You Talk or Write for Different People

One crucial way to ensure people understand what you're saying or writing is to change how you talk or write based on who you're talking to. This is important for both speaking and writing.

Here are some tips to help you do this:

- **Communicate at the level of the people you're talking to.** Not everyone has the same level of knowledge and understanding. If you speak or write too simply or in a too complicated way, people may be confused or lose interest. Try to understand what your audience knows about the topic before you start.

For instance, when discussing a movie with a friend who hasn't seen it, you might begin with the basics, explaining the plot and the main characters. On the other hand, if your friend has just watched the movie, you can skip the introduction and dive into discussing your favorite parts.

- **Keep it simple.** Use language and examples your audience can easily understand.

- **Use examples that people can relate to.** This lets you connect what people already know with the information you share. This makes it easier for them to understand your message.

In summary, changing your communication style to fit your audience is crucial, as it helps you connect with listeners, build trust, and share your message clearly and effectively.

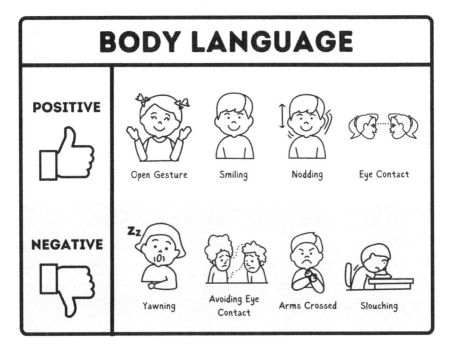

Body language is integral to effective communication and tells us much about someone's feelings, even when they don't say anything. Reading someone's body language can help you understand the people around you and make communicating easier.

Here are some tips on how to read body language:

- **Pay attention to facial expressions:** Facial expressions are one of the most telling forms of nonverbal communication. They can tell you a lot about how someone feels in the moment, such as whether they're happy, sad, angry, or anxious. Paying attention to subtle changes in a person's facial expressions can give clues to their emotional state.

- **Observe body positioning:** Pay attention to how someone is positioned in relation to you. Are they leaning toward you or away from you? Is their posture open or closed off? Open body language signals that a person feels comfortable and relaxed. In contrast, closed-off body language, like crossing your arms, can indicate discomfort or hostility.

- **Pay attention to gestures:** Gestures provide important clues into how a person feels and thinks. *For example, noticing someone's hand gestures can tell whether they are excited about something or frustrated.*

- **Use your own body language:** You can also use body language to your advantage in communication. Maintaining eye contact, keeping an open posture, and using hand gestures during conversations can help others feel more comfortable and show that you are engaged.

By learning how to read and respond to body language effectively, you'll be able to communicate more effectively and build stronger relationships. With this knowledge, you'll be better prepared to confidently navigate middle school and succeed!

SECTION 5: HOW TO BUILD HEALTHY RELATIONSHIPS, RESOLVE CONFLICTS, AND SET BOUNDARIES

As a middle schooler, navigating friends and relationships can sometimes be tricky. There is often pressure to be part of a group, and many students are still figuring out who they are and where they belong. This can cause worries about fitting in and fears about being left out.

Managing your social life and relationships becomes much easier when you know how to build healthy relationships, resolve conflicts peacefully, and set appropriate boundaries.

Healthy relationships are built on caring for each other, trust, empathy, respect, and talking openly. Whether with family, friends, teachers, or neighbors, having these good communication skills will help you build strong connections.

Empathy and Understanding Make Friendships Better

Understanding how others feel is an essential skill that helps you to connect with people and their experiences. It is something that makes a great friend.

So, what is empathy?

Empathy is the ability to share someone else's feelings and experiences by imagining how it would feel to be in their situation.

This means understanding how your words and actions affect others and recognizing when someone needs space or help.

The active listening skills we covered earlier in this chapter play a significant role in being empathetic. Here are some tips for practicing empathy:

- **Listen carefully:** When someone is talking, make eye contact and give them your full attention.

- **Put yourself in their shoes:** When listening, imagine how the other person might feel or what they might be experiencing.

- **Be kind:** Show kindness and compassion by showing concern for the other person's feelings.

- **Offer to help:** If a friend shares a problem, tell them you care and ask if you can help.

- **Be respectful:** Always treat the other person with respect.

Empathy and understanding create an environment where everyone feels valued, respected, and heard. It creates a positive and supportive environment that's good for everyone.

How to Resolve Conflicts Peacefully and Effectively

Despite your best efforts, you will experience conflicts and arguments as you get older, even with your best friends. Being able to resolve disputes peacefully and effectively is a valuable skill.

Here are some tips for peacefully resolving conflicts:

- **Use your active listening skills.** Try to understand the other person's perspective. Listen closely to what they're saying, recognize and acknowledge their feelings, and ask them questions.

- **Stay calm.** Remain calm, be respectful, and avoid using critical or judging language.

- **Identify areas of agreement or shared interests.** Try to focus on these shared interests when discussing the conflict.

- **Talk through potential solutions to the conflict.** Be open-minded, consider all ideas, and be willing to compromise.

- **Choose a solution and move on.** After discussing solutions, choose one that works for both of you, then move on with your friendship.

- **Seek help.** If you're unable to peacefully resolve a conflict, seek advice from a trusted adult, such as a teacher or parent.

Remember that resolving conflicts peacefully takes practice and patience. Fortunately, good communication skills and a willingness to work together will often lead to a solution that works for everyone.

Setting Healthy Boundaries

Creating and maintaining healthy boundaries is essential for building relationships. Setting boundaries gives you the power to make decisions based on your beliefs. It helps to build a healthy balance in relationships.

But first, what exactly are boundaries?

Boundaries are rules or limits that you can use to let people know what you are uncomfortable with and how you would like to be treated.

The most common types of boundaries relate to your body, feelings, friendships, or time.

TYPES OF BOUNDARIES

BODY BOUNDARIES

Are about your body and personal space. You have the right to say "no" if someone tries to touch you or invades your space in ways that make you uncomfortable.

EMOTIONAL BOUNDARIES

Are about respecting your emotions and privacy. For example, not making someone share personal information they don't want to discuss.

FRIENDSHIP BOUNDARIES

Are about how people behave with others. For example, not getting involved in conversations or gossiping about other people.

TIME BOUNDARIES

Are about the time you spend with others. For example, taking time away from friends is okay to spend time with your family or on other personal interests.

Here are some tips for setting boundaries:

- **Know what makes you uncomfortable:** Think about what makes you uncomfortable. This might include things that have happened to you before or things you don't want to happen in the future.

- **Consider how boundaries can help:** Consider how setting boundaries might make you feel more at ease.

- **Create a list:** List the boundaries you want to establish.

- **Communicate:** Tell others about your boundaries. It's good to tell others and be upfront about your boundaries. *For example, "I don't like it when you borrow my books without asking," or "It makes me uncomfortable when you hug me without asking."*

- **Stand up for yourself:** If something makes you uncomfortable, don't let other people pressure you or make you feel guilty about your boundaries.

- **Consider the situation:** Remember your boundaries can vary for the different people in your life, like your family and close friends, compared to those you don't know well.

Let's look at some examples of what setting boundaries might look like:

> *Example 1: You feel uncomfortable talking about your personal life with someone. So you tell them that this topic is not something you want to discuss and explain you'd rather talk about something else.*
>
> *Example 2: Someone asks you to do something, but you don't have the time. You explain that you're happy to help, but you don't have the time on this occasion.*
>
> *Example 3: A friend asks to copy your homework. You explain to them that this is not something you're comfortable doing but offer to help them understand the topic.*

Setting boundaries can be difficult and takes practice and patience. Still, it is an important skill to learn for your safety and well-being. It helps you build healthy relationships, protects you from unhealthy friendships, and helps to build self-confidence.

SECTION 6: PUTTING IT INTO PRACTICE

Now that you know how essential good communication skills are for doing well in school, after-school activities, and friendships, it's time to start using what you've learned. By working on these skills when listening, speaking, writing, or using body language, you can improve and become a superstar communicator, helping you achieve your goals in life.

Here are some takeaways to improve your communication skills:

- **Practice:** Work on your speaking skills during conversations and when speaking in front of a group.

- **Pay attention to body language:** Develop your nonverbal communication skills by paying attention to body language, facial expressions, and tone of voice.

- **Consider your audience:** Practice writing or speaking to different people.

- **Be thoughtful:** Consider what makes a healthy relationship and how you can improve your friendships.

- **Be empathetic:** Practice empathy and understanding when listening to others, especially if they think differently.

- **Resolve conflicts:** Do your best to resolve disputes peacefully and effectively.

- **Set boundaries:** Determine the boundaries you want to set and ensure others respect them.

As you work on these things, note what you're learning. That way, you can see your progress in becoming a superstar communicator!

NON-VERBAL COMMUNICATION

Communication is more than just words - it includes actions and body language too. Can you guess how people are feeling by their actions? Give it a try!

WHAT ARE THEY FEELING?

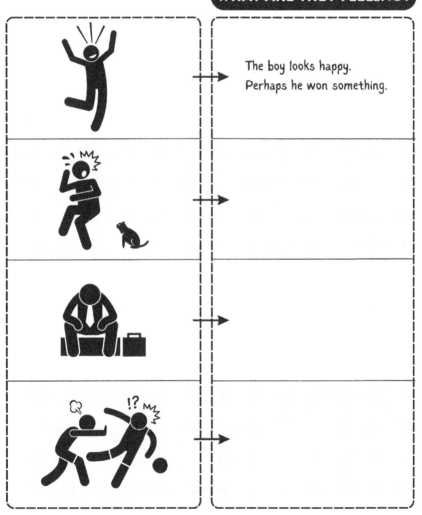

The boy looks happy.
Perhaps he won something.

CHAPTER 5:

THINKING BIG: YOUR GROWTH MINDSET

"Believe you can, and you're halfway there."
— Theodore Roosevelt, 26th US President.

Have you ever had a school assignment that was so hard you wanted to quit? Maybe it was in a subject you've always struggled with. Perhaps you thought that, since you've been struggling with it for so long, you'll never really understand it or get good grades.

If this sounds familiar, you're not alone. Many middle schoolers feel like this, especially when faced with a challenging task. But what if you could overcome these feelings? What if you could see tough assignments as challenges and learning opportunities? That's where a growth mindset comes into play.

A growth mindset is a way of thinking that helps you deal with challenges and failures in a positive way that can ultimately help lead to success. In this chapter, you'll find practical tips and real-life examples to show you what a growth mindset is. We'll explore the importance of having a growth mindset and give you practical strategies and exercises to help you develop this powerful thinking.

Topics we'll cover in this chapter include:

● What is a growth mindset?

● The difference between a growth mindset and a fixed mindset

● Strategies for developing a growth mindset

● Embracing challenges and learning from mistakes

● Using positive self-talk

Ready? Let's get started!

SECTION 1: WHAT IS A GROWTH MINDSET AND WHY IS IT IMPORTANT?

First, let's define a growth mindset:

> A growth mindset is a belief that our abilities and talents can be developed and improved through practice, hard work, and the attitude that we can do better.

In other words, having a growth mindset means that, even if you aren't very good at something right now, you believe that you can improve with enough effort and practice. *For example, suppose you struggle with algebra but have a growth mindset. In that case, you think studying and practicing will help you get better grades.*

A growth mindset helps you become a better student. Instead of giving up when something is difficult, a person with a growth mindset will see challenges as opportunities to learn and grow.

People with a growth mindset are hungry to learn and improve. They set goals for themselves and work hard to achieve them. They know that success is not just down to natural talent but that it comes to those who continue to put in the effort.

A Growth Mindset vs. a Fixed Mindset

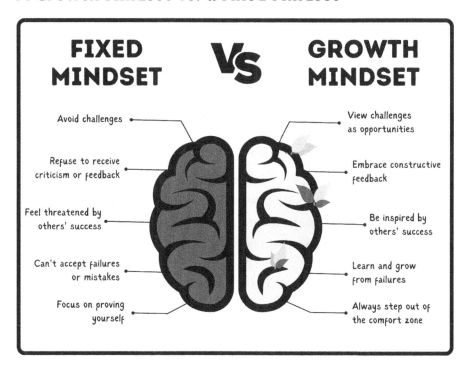

A fixed mindset is the opposite of a growth mindset. People with fixed mindsets believe your talent, intelligence, and abilities are fixed. They give up easily if they find something challenging and say, "I'll never be good at this," instead of trying to improve or learn new skills. With a growth mindset, anything is possible with effort and hard work.

Here are some characteristics of growth vs. fixed mindset:

Growth mindset:

- Believes that you can improve at something through practice and effort.
- View challenges as opportunities to learn and grow.
- Not afraid to make mistakes. Instead, they see mistakes as part of the learning process.

Fixed mindset:

- Believes that talent, intelligence, and abilities are fixed.
- Avoids activities that require new skills, fearing failure.
- Gives up quickly when things get challenging.

The difference between a growth mindset and a fixed mindset can enormously impact people's lives. A growth mindset opens doors to opportunities, new challenges, and wonderful experiences, while a fixed mindset can hold them back.

Let's explore some of the benefits of having a growth mindset.

The Benefits of Developing a Growth Mindset

As a middle schooler, there are many benefits to developing a growth mindset.

Some of the key benefits include:

- **Improved self-confidence:** If you believe you can improve at something through practice and effort, you'll feel more confident in your ability to do well, giving you the courage to take on new challenges.

- **Motivation:** With a growth mindset, you'll be motivated and inspired by the opportunity to learn, practice, work, and improve. As a result, you're more likely to take on challenging projects and be open to new experiences.

- **See failures as opportunities to learn:** A growth mindset helps you see setbacks as learning opportunities instead of failures. This mindset can help you bounce back from setbacks and keep going, even when things get tough.

- **Improved grades:** Research has shown that students with a growth mindset perform better in school than those with a fixed mindset. Motivated by the challenge to learn something new, they are more likely to go the extra mile to complete challenging assignments, resulting in greater success at school.

- **More resilient and adaptable:** As a person with a growth mindset, you'll be more open to feedback because you always look for ways to improve. As a result, you'll be able to handle conflicts and adapt to change.

In summary, developing a growth mindset can significantly impact your middle school life, which can help set you up for success in college and life.

SECTION 2: HOW TO DEVELOP A GROWTH MINDSET

Developing a growth mindset takes time and practice. Think of it like going to a gym—you won't get fit overnight, but if you go every day, you'll slowly start to see progress. Here are some tips on how to develop a growth mindset:

- **Challenge yourself:** Try new things, take on complex projects, and do activities that push you out of your comfort zone. This will help you learn new skills, build self-confidence and overcome fears of failure.

- **Don't give up:** Even when things seem difficult, keep trying and do your best to push through obstacles and setbacks. Remember, anything is possible if you work hard.

- **Learn from your mistakes:** Nobody enjoys making mistakes, but instead of seeing them as failures, see them as part of the learning process. When you make a mistake, think about what you can learn to help you improve in the future.

- **Practice positive self-talk:** Use positive self-talk and focus on your strengths rather than your weaknesses or failures from the past. *For example, instead of saying: "I'm not good at math," try saying, "I find math tricky, but I'm getting better!"* This will help you build confidence and motivation.

- **Set achievable goals:** Setting achievable goals gives you a target. Try setting long-term goals that challenge you. Celebrate each success along the way to stay motivated.

- **Ask for feedback:** Ask teachers, parents, or classmates how you are getting on. Use the feedback they give you as an opportunity to learn and improve.

Developing a growth mindset takes time, practice, and effort. By embracing challenges, persisting through obstacles, and learning from your mistakes, you can develop a growth mindset that will help you succeed in school and life.

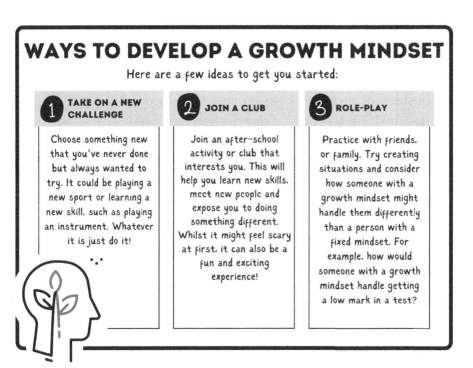

WAYS TO DEVELOP A GROWTH MINDSET

Here are a few ideas to get you started:

1 TAKE ON A NEW CHALLENGE

Choose something new that you've never done but always wanted to try. It could be playing a new sport or learning a new skill, such as playing an instrument. Whatever it is just do it!

2 JOIN A CLUB

Join an after-school activity or club that interests you. This will help you learn new skills, meet new people and expose you to doing something different. Whilst it might feel scary at first, it can also be a fun and exciting experience!

3 ROLE-PLAY

Practice with friends, or family. Try creating situations and consider how someone with a growth mindset might handle them differently than a person with a fixed mindset. For example, how would someone with a growth mindset handle getting a low mark in a test?

SECTION 3: HOW TO EMBRACE CHALLENGES

"If there is no struggle, there is no progress."
– Frederick Douglass, American social reformer.

Seeing setbacks as opportunities for learning and growth is integral to developing a growth mindset. For example, instead of giving up when you don't understand something in class, use it to learn something about a new topic. If you can embrace challenges rather than avoid them, you'll develop self-confidence and be more successful in everything you do.

Tips for Facing Challenges with a Growth Mindset

- **Think positively:** Instead of looking at challenges as setbacks, ask yourself, "What can I learn from this?" or "How can I improve."

- **Change negative self-talk:** When you are struggling, instead of saying, "I have no idea how to do this. I give up!" try saying, "I haven't figured this out yet, but I will."

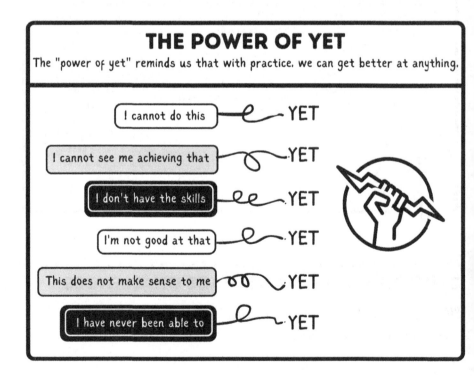

THE POWER OF YET
The "power of yet" reminds us that with practice, we can get better at anything.

I cannot do this	YET
I cannot see me achieving that	YET
I don't have the skills	YET
I'm not good at that	YET
This does not make sense to me	YET
I have never been able to	YET

- **Focus on effort:** Keep your focus on the effort and hard work you put in rather than worrying about the outcome. When achieving success, the effort is often more important than the result.

- **Keep trying:** Progress can sometimes be slow, especially when you hit an obstacle. But don't give up. Remember that the only way to reach a challenging goal is to keep trying.

SECTION 4: HOW TO LEARN FROM MISTAKES

Everyone makes mistakes, and that's okay. Mistakes are an essential part of the learning process. No one ever succeeds without making mistakes along the way! It's how you deal with mistakes that counts. You'll become a more confident and successful learner by using mistakes as opportunities to learn and grow.

Here are some ways to learn from mistakes:

- **Own your mistakes:** The best way to learn from mistakes is to own up to them. Mistakes can be frustrating and embarrassing, and it's sometimes difficult to admit when you've made them. But it's essential to face your mistakes and learn from them.

- **Use your mistakes:** Your mistakes usually highlight areas where you need to study more, develop new skills, or do something different. *For example, if you get a low mark on a test, you probably need to study more or use another method.*

- **Practice makes perfect:** Learning from mistakes often takes time. *For example, learning to play a musical instrument takes hours of training and a willingness to make many mistakes. Still, every false note takes you one step closer to success.*

Finally, it's important to remember that everyone makes mistakes. Don't worry too much about making mistakes; they happen to the best of us! Learn from them, move on, and don't repeat the same mistakes.

How to Develop a Positive Approach to Failure

"I haven't failed; I have just found 10,000 ways that don't work."
— Thomas Edison (inventor of the lightbulb).

Failing is just part of life. You will fail. A lot.

Developing a positive approach to failure is integral to learning and personal growth. It took famous inventor Thomas Edison more than a thousand unsuccessful attempts to invent the lightbulb. But instead of viewing failure as a negative experience, he regarded every failure as a step closer to his goal.

When you fail at something, try to understand what went wrong and what you can do differently next time. And remember, failure is usually only temporary. With hard work and persistence, you will find a way to overcome whatever is holding you back.

Remember, every failure is a step toward success.

. . . .
SECTION 5: HOW TO USE POSITIVE SELF-TALK

Positive self-talk is the process of talking to yourself positively. It can be in your head through supportive thoughts or out loud with words of encouragement.

Examples of positive self-talk include:
"I can do this!"
"I'm going to try hard to succeed."

Examples of negative self-talk include:
"There's no way I can do this!"
"I give up!"

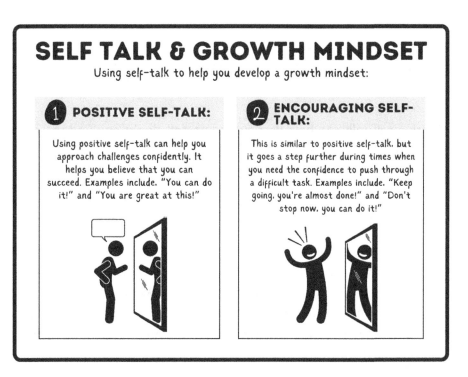

Positive self-talk is an essential part of developing a growth mindset. How you talk to yourself will affect your mindset and influence how you approach challenges.

Here are some ways to use positive self-talk:

- **Be positive:** Replace negative thoughts with positive ones. *For example: "I can't do this" with "I'm going to do my best to get it done."*

- **Focus on your achievements:** Instead of focusing on what you haven't done, focus on what you have already achieved. *For example, instead of thinking: "I've got so much work to do, and I'm already behind," think, "Look at what I've done already."*

- **Celebrate your wins:** Don't be too hard on yourself. *For example, instead of saying: "That wasn't good enough," say, "I worked hard and did my best."*

Positive self-talk can help you overcome self-doubt and find the courage to push ahead when things are tough, which will help you face challenges at middle school and beyond.

Be Kind to Yourself

While learning to develop a growth mindset, you will likely encounter setbacks. Remember that nobody is perfect. Everyone makes mistakes—it's just part of the learning process. As you have learned in this chapter, how you react to setbacks matters. Instead of giving up, just remember you have the power to grow and improve if you keep working hard.

A Growth Mindset Leads to Lifelong Learning

Building a growth mindset now can lead to a lifetime of learning and achievement. Learning doesn't end once you finish school. Many companies need employees to learn new skills to keep up with technological changes and business operations.

With a growth mindset, you can turn mistakes and failures into valuable lessons and achieve things that you once thought were impossible. Keep an open mind, embrace challenges, and never stop learning and growing!

. . . .

SECTION 7: PUTTING IT INTO PRACTICE

In this chapter, we've discussed how a growth mindset can help you succeed in middle school and beyond.

Here are some ideas for practicing a growth mindset in your daily life:

- **Embrace challenges:** Embrace challenges as opportunities to learn and grow.

- **Be open to new experiences:** We learn and grow from pushing ourselves outside our comfort zone. Say "yes" to new experiences and learn from them.

- **Learn from your mistakes:** Instead of seeing them as failures, see them as opportunities to learn and grow.

- **Invite feedback:** Seek out feedback and use it to improve.

- **Keep trying:** Don't give up. Remember, the only way to reach your goals is to keep going.

- **Use Positive self-talk:** Discover the power of positive self-talk.

- **Choose the right support network:** Surround yourself with people who encourage and support your growth.

By using these strategies, you'll slowly develop your growth mindset, opening doors and ensuring you lead a successful and fulfilling life.

YOU'RE AMAZING!

Be kind to yourself and think differently. How could you use positive self-talk and a growth mindset in these example scenarios?

INSTEAD OF SAYING...	TELL YOURSELF...
I messed up and now I look stupid!	I worked hard, and didn't get it right this time, but nobody is perfect, and I have learnt from my mistakes.
I can't do that, it's too hard.	
I will never be good at that.	
I'm scared I'll look stupid if I try that sport.	
I hate this project.	
I know I'm just going to fail.	
I don't understand this.	
I'll let them down if I change my mind.	

CHAPTER 6:

EMOTIONAL INTELLIGENCE: UNDERSTANDING FEELINGS

"When awareness is brought to an emotion, power is brought to your life."
– Tara Meyer Robson, mind-body expert and author.

You may already know about intelligence, but have you heard about emotional intelligence?

Emotional intelligence, or EQ, is vital for developing the skills needed to succeed as a middle schooler and beyond. Recognizing and managing your emotions and understanding others will improve your friendships, help you make better decisions, and manage stress.

In this chapter, we'll explore ways to build your emotional intelligence so you can be successful in middle school and beyond.

Topics we'll cover in this chapter include:

● Understanding emotional intelligence
● Controlling strong emotions
● Self-Motivation and goal-setting

- Empathy and social skills
- Building emotional resilience

Ready? Let's get started!

SECTION 1: UNDERSTANDING EMOTIONAL INTELLIGENCE

Middle school can be an emotional time. There's a lot to deal with—and with so many changes in your body, you might feel like you're on a rollercoaster of emotions. You might feel happy, sad, social, or introverted some days. But that's okay. All of these emotions are a normal part of life.

The key is learning how to recognize, understand, and manage your emotions and understand the feelings of others so that you can respond to situations effectively and thoughtfully.

First off, what does emotional intelligence really mean?

Emotional intelligence is being able to recognize, understand, and manage your own emotions and understand and be considerate of the feelings of others.

For example, if someone is mean to you. With emotional intelligence, you can pause, look at the situation and understand how the person is feeling and why they were mean to you. Then, instead of reacting angrily, you can respond calmly and thoughtfully.

Emotional intelligence includes a range of abilities, including self-aware-ness, self-regulation, self-motivation, empathy, and other social skills. Together, they help you understand and manage your emotions, making your life run smoothly.

Emotional Intelligence Skills

Emotional intelligence has five main skill sets. These are:

- **Self-awareness:** Understanding your emotions and behaviors and how they affect others.

- **Self-regulation:** Being able to control your emotions and behaviors.

- **Motivation:** Being motivated to work towards goals.

- **Empathy:** Understanding the emotions and feelings of others.

- **Social skills:** Communicating effectively, building positive rela-tionships, and working with others.

Developing these five skills will help you build your own emotions and behaviors, as well as an understanding of others, allowing you to achieve success in your school and personal life.

Emotional Intelligence in Everyday Life

Now you understand emotional intelligence, let's explore how it can be used in everyday life.

Middle schoolers with emotional intelligence find it easier to focus on schoolwork, manage time effectively, and work well with others. They can better handle everyday situations, including:

- Handling challenges and setbacks.

- Building relationships with friends, parents, and teachers.
- Managing stress, emotions, and behavior positively.
- Working in teams.

SECTION 2: HOW TO UNDERSTAND AND CONTROL STRONG EMOTIONS

The first step is developing self-awareness and self-regulation.

Self-awareness means learning to be aware of your emotions and how they affect you and others.

Self-regulation means learning how to control or regulate those emotions to react calmly to any person or situation.

Tips on developing self-awareness:

- **How do you feel?** Take time each day to check in with yourself and reflect on your feelings and thoughts. Ask yourself, "How am I feeling right now?" and "What might be causing those feelings?"

- **Record your emotions:** In a journal, note any strong feelings or emotions and how they affect your behavior. *For example, ask yourself, "How did that feeling affect my relationships with my friends?"*

- **Record your triggers:** Identity what causes you to feel strong emotions. Being aware of situations that trigger strong feelings makes managing them easier. *For example, if talking to a friend makes you feel anxious, ask yourself why that may be.*

Journaling and mindfulness are two essential tools you can use in your journey to improve emotional intelligence.

Journaling

Journaling is an excellent tool for recording your thoughts and feelings and practicing self-awareness.

Most people use a notepad or journal to write about their feelings, experiences, goals, and challenges. Still, you can also use digital journaling apps.

You can better understand yourself and your behavior in different situations by writing down your thoughts and emotions. By writing honestly, you can see patterns in your behavior and identify areas of your life you want to change.

How to journal in four simple steps:

1 **Set a time:** Set a time in your day to write in your journal—start off with 10 minutes, to begin with.

2 **Write your thoughts:** Write down your thoughts and feelings. Be honest with yourself; it's not about judging or coming up with solutions. It's about expressing how you feel.

3 **Read what you've written:** Review what you wrote and reflect on how the events or emotions made you feel. Ask yourself: "How did the emotions affect my behavior."

4 **Take action:** Regularly writing and reflecting on your emotions will help you identify patterns. Try to take action to make positive changes.

Mindfulness

Mindfulness is another great tool to help you develop emotional intelligence.

Mindfulness involves being fully aware of everything happening inside you, like your thoughts, feelings, body sensations, and around you, without judging or worrying about what has happened in the past or might happen in the future.

Think of it like a pause button. When you practice mindfulness, you press pause on the world and can take a step back from what is happening at that moment.

> *For example, imagine you are having a disagreement with a friend. When you practice mindfulness, you can recognize the feeling of anger. Instead of being led by your rage and reacting impulsively, you can pause, take a deep breath, and think clearly before you speak.*

There are many ways to practice mindfulness. Here are a few you can use:

1. **Focus on your breath:** One of the simplest is taking a few minutes each day to focus on your breath, body, and senses. This can be done in the morning, evening, or any time you need to become more relaxed.

2. **Be aware of your feelings:** Notice how you feel in different situations. It's not about judging them as good or bad, just about being able to identify them.

3. **Take in the world around you:** Look at the world around you. Really take it in. Try to notice the small details like

the colors of a tree, the shapes of the leaves, or the movement of the branches.

4 **Be grateful:** Take a moment to think about someone or something positive for which you are thankful. You could mark this down in your journal.

5 **Enjoy mindful activities:** Yoga, meditation, walking, drawing, and coloring are all activities that can help you develop mindfulness.

By practicing mindfulness, you can develop greater self-awareness—noticing your thoughts, feelings, and bodily sensations. This can help you make better decisions and build your emotional intelligence.

Strategies for Controlling Strong Emotions

As a middle schooler, many things can cause you to feel emotional. When you least expect it, someone might say or do something that makes you laugh, cry, or fly into an emotional rage. When emotions run high, things can be said or done that you might regret later.

Here are some strategies you can use to help you control these strong emotions:

1 **Understand your triggers:** One of the first steps in understanding and controlling strong emotions is to learn what causes them.

Ask yourself, "Why am I feeling this way?" Take note of situations, people, and events that cause strong emotions. Once you can identify these triggers, you can start to work on the causes of your feelings.

Basic guide to...

MINDFULNESS MEDITATION

This meditation technique involves focusing your attention on the present moment without judging your thoughts, emotions or feelings.

1. Find a quiet space without distractions to practice.

2. Sit in a comfortable position that allows you to be alert but also relaxed and upright.

3. Lightly close your eyes.

4. Breathe in through your nose, expanding your belly with air and releasing through your nose. Perhaps let a few long inhales out through your mouth, as well.

5. Be with the thoughts that come to mind but do not attach to them. Focus on breathing and try to simply notice whatever is the feeling you experience, in the moment.

6. Keep breathing in and out, focusing on your breath. Try to do this for 5-10 minutes every day.

2 **Pause, take a deep breath, and think:** Often, just pausing for a few seconds, taking a deep breath, and giving yourself time to think about a situation is enough to calm your body down. This allows you to decide how you respond rather than being led by your emotions.

3 **Put yourself in their shoes:** Once you've paused and reset. Try to think about the other person. Why are they behaving this way? What are they feeling? Thinking from the other person's perspective can help you see the situation differently. Which can help you make a less emotional response.

4 **Develop coping mechanisms:** A coping mechanism is something you do that helps you to de-stress and manage your emotions. Let's explore some coping mechanisms and see how they can help you control powerful emotions.

- **Mindfulness and meditation:** Practicing mindfulness and being present in the moment can help you connect with your body, and emotions can help you to remain calm in stressful situations.

- **Exercise:** Have you ever felt better after doing some exercise? Perhaps it was a workout, a run, or cycling home from school. Exercise is known to improve your mood and help reduce stress. Find a physical activity you enjoy, such as playing a sport, dancing, or walking.

- **Talk:** Talking to a friend or trusted adult, such as a parent, teacher, or counselor, can help to clarify emotions, build possible solutions and help to reduce personal stress.

- **Creative activities:** Creative expression, such as drawing, writing, or making music, can be calming and are an excellent way to take your mind off stressful situations. Try different outlets for your creativity to find the ones you enjoy the most.

By practicing these strategies, you can develop strong emotional regulation skills that will serve you well in middle school and beyond.

. . . .

SECTION 3: HOW TO DEVELOP SELF-MOTIVATION

As you enter middle school, it's time to start setting your own goals.

This can be a challenging yet exciting step in your life, as the goals you set now will significantly impact your success. When you were in grade school, your parents and teachers had specific expectations for what they wanted you to achieve. Now that it is up to you, you must consider what you want for yourself.

Use Self-Motivation to Achieve Your Goals

What do you enjoy doing? What are you good at? What are your passions?

These are questions that will help you shape your future goals.

When you are passionate about something, staying motivated and putting in the hard work and practice is easier. And that's what self-motivation is all about. Self-motivation is fuelled by your own passions and interests. It comes from within and drives you to work hard to achieve your goals.

When you are self-motivated to do something, you'll be more likely to stick with it, put in the effort, and enjoy working towards your goal. It's a great feeling to do something because you love it rather than because you feel like you have to!

When you can motivate yourself from within and keep going even when faced with challenges, setbacks, and obstacles, you will be unstoppable!

How to Stay Self-Motivated

Here are some simple steps you can take to stay motivated and continue developing your emotional intelligence:

1. **Identify what motivates you:** Think about your self-motivation. What is it that drives you? Use this as inspiration when facing setbacks.

2. **Set goals:** Set yourself achievable goals that are realistic and challenging.

3. **Celebrate wins:** When you tick off those small tasks, celebrate them. Take time to enjoy your successes and triumphs.

You can stay motivated and achieve your goals by adopting these three simple steps.

. . . .

SECTION 4: HOW TO BUILD EMPATHY AND SOCIAL AWARENESS

Empathy, active listening, and the other social skills you learned earlier in this book are some of the most essential parts of emotional intelligence. As you may remember, empathy is about putting yourself in other people's shoes to understand their feelings and how they see the world. Using empathy and your social skills helps you form friendships, navigate conflicts and develop better communication skills.

Here are some further tips for developing empathy and social awareness:

- **Listen actively:** Listen carefully to what the other person is saying.

- **Ask questions:** Ask questions to clarify, and show understanding and interest.

- **Be open-minded:** Respect the other person's views and try to understand where they stand, even if you disagree with them.

- **Watch your body language:** Be mindful of your body language. Crossing your arms or being distracted shows you are not interested. Eye contact or nodding your head shows the other person you are fully engaged.

OTHER WAYS TO DEVELOP
SOCIAL AWARENESS

 ### INCREASE YOUR CULTURAL AWARENESS
Today it's more important than ever to be able to communicate effectively with people from different cultures and backgrounds. Seek out opportunities to connect with people from diverse backgrounds.

 ### VOLUNTEER
Doing volunteer work can help you develop empathy for the people you help. Consider volunteering at a local charity, school, or community organization.

 ### LEARN TO BE A LEADER
Middle school is a great time to develop your leadership skills. These skills are valuable in many areas of life, including school, extracurricular activities, and future careers.

SECTION 5: HOW TO BUILD EMOTIONAL RESILIENCE

Building emotional resilience is integral to developing emotional intelligence for middle schoolers.

What is emotional resilience?

Emotional resilience is the ability to cope with life's ups and downs. It's about being able to bounce back from setbacks, cope with stress and face challenging situations with confidence and strength.

The skills we have already covered in this chapter go a long way toward developing emotional resilience. But let's look at a few more tips to help build emotional strength:

- **Learn to make mistakes:** That might sound strange, but as you already know, making mistakes is a healthy way to learn and improve.

- **Allow others to make mistakes:** If it's okay for you to make mistakes, you must accept when others make them. Remember that nobody is perfect.

- **Look after your mental and physical health:** Ensure you get enough sleep, eat healthily, exercise regularly, and, most importantly, allow yourself time to relax.

- **Express yourself:** Don't bottle up feelings and emotions. Talk to someone you trust, or write down how you feel in your journal.

Following these tips and the other skills covered in the chapter, you can develop the emotional resilience to survive and thrive in middle school and beyond.

Strategies for Managing Stress and Adversity

No matter how emotionally intelligent you are, as a middle schooler, you will face challenges along the way. These might come from::

● Schoolwork pressure

● Peer pressure

● Friendship groups

● Family issues

● Overloaded schedules

● Stressful events in the news

Whatever it is, stress can feel like a daily reality. Here are some tips to help you manage stress:

● **Identify what's causing the stress:** Often, it is helpful to identify the source of the stress to find possible solutions.

● **Take care of yourself:** Remember to prioritize healthy habits, such as getting enough sleep, eating healthy meals, and meditating or engaging in physical activity.

● **Get outside and take a break:** Sometimes, returning to nature is enough to destress, relax and unwind.

● **Use your journal:** Research has shown that writing about things you are grateful for or positive affirmations can help reduce stress and anxiety.

- **Ask for help:** Talk to your family, friends, or a trusted adult. They can provide guidance, perspective, or simply a non-judgmental ear!

Remember that learning to effectively manage stress is an ongoing process. It is essential to be patient and keep practicing these strategies over time.

SECTION 6: PUTTING IT INTO PRACTICE

In this chapter, we've looked at emotional intelligence, including learning, recognizing, and understanding your emotions and being considerate of others. Now it's time to put what you've learned into practice. Here are some tips for getting started:

- **Check in with yourself:** Take time each day to reflect on your thoughts and feelings.

- **Journal:** Record your thoughts and feelings to become more self-aware.

- **Identify your triggers:** List down what triggers your strong emotions and feelings.

- **Develop coping mechanisms:** Try using different coping tools, such as exercise, meditation, talking, or creative activities.

- **Identify what motivates you:** Think about your self-motivation. What is it that drives you? Use this as inspiration when facing setbacks.

- **Identify causes of anxiety:** Identify the source of the stress to find possible solutions.

- **Take care of yourself:** Prioritize healthy habits, such as getting enough sleep, eating healthy meals, and meditating or engaging in physical activity.

By adopting these strategies and the tips in this chapter, you will be able to recognize and understand your emotions and the feelings of others and better navigate middle school and beyond.

DAILY JOURNALING

Let's start your day by identifying what you feel at the moment. Write down how you are feeling right now.

What's one thing you're excited about today and why?

Is there something on your mind or something that happened today that you'd like to write about?

What is the one thing that you can do today that will help you stay positive?

Let's end your journal with three things you are grateful for today.

1. _____
2. _____
3. _____

CHAPTER 7:

SELF CARE: TAKING CARE OF YOU

"It is so important to take time for yourself and find clarity. The most important relationship is the one you have with yourself."
— Diane von Furstenberg, fashion designer.

While doing everything you can to succeed at middle school, it is vital to make time for self-care. Good self-care habits can help improve physical and mental health, manage stress, and maintain well-being.

In this chapter, we'll explore self-care, why it's essential, and how you can develop healthy habits. We'll also provide tips for looking after yourself in different areas of your life, such as physical health, mental health, relationships, and leisure time.

Topics we'll cover in this chapter include:

- Understanding self-care
- Physical self-care
- Mental and emotional self-care

- Social self-care
- Spiritual self-care

If you're ready to start taking better care of yourself, let's get going!

SECTION 1: UNDERSTANDING SELF-CARE

First, let's make sure we understand what self-care is and why it's so important:

Self-care is about looking after your physical, mental, emotional, and spiritual well-being.

In other words, it's about learning to look after yourself, making time for yourself, and doing things that you enjoy and that make you happy. This includes your basic needs, like getting a good night's sleep, eating healthily, exercising, and activities that make you feel happy and fulfilled, like spending time with friends, listening to music, or watching a film.

Why should you prioritize self-care? Because when you take good care of yourself, you'll be better at everything you do. You'll be more focused, have more energy, and be more productive in school and other activities.

The importance of self-care can't be overstated—it plays a crucial role in helping manage stress, build resilience, stay healthy and happy, succeed at school, and enjoy life. So with that in mind, let's jump into the different aspects of self-care...

SECTION 2: HOW TO DEVELOP PHYSICAL SELF-CARE

Physical self-care is all about taking care of your body. This includes eating nutritious food, exercising regularly, and getting a good night's sleep.

Let's take a look at each area in a bit more detail.

Good Nutrition Fuels Your Mind and Body

Your body is like an engine—it needs fuel to run correctly. And that fuel comes from the food you put into it. Just as you won't put the wrong fuel into a gasoline engine, if you want your engine (body) to run efficiently, you must give it the right fuel.

This means eating a balanced and nutritious diet that includes food from all the different food groups. These include fruits, vegetables, whole grains, lean proteins, and healthy fats. Eating healthily will help you feel energized, alert, and ready to tackle anything.

Here are some ways to make sure you are eating healthy:

- **Eat plenty of fruit and veg:** Eat at least five servings of fruits and vegetables daily. Include as many different colored fruits and vegetables in your diet as possible, as each has a different balance of vitamins and minerals your body needs.

- **Include whole grains:** Whole grain products are foods made from the entire grain of wheat, oats, barley, rice, etc. Whole grains are important because they provide fiber, which helps your digestive system work properly.

- **Get enough protein:** Protein is vital in a healthy diet. Meat has protein, as do fish, beans, lentils, and tofu.

- **Don't forget healthy fats:** Fats are found in nuts, seeds, avocados, and other foods. They are essential for brain function, as well as your overall health.

- **Limit sugary snacks:** Sugary drinks, candy, and other unhealthy snacks may be tasty, but they should be limited. Instead, stick to healthy snacks like fruit, nuts, and vegetables.

- **Drink plenty of water:** Water is vital to help your body stay hydrated and function properly.

HOW MUCH WATER SHOULD YOU DRINK?

AGES 4-8	AGES 9-13	AGES 14+
GIRLS		
5	7	8
BOYS		
5	8	11

Exercise Makes You Feel Good

Exercise plays an essential role in physical self-care. Exercise helps your body build muscle, strengthen bones, and improve breathing and circulation.

Exercise has mental health benefits, as well. Exercising regularly helps reduce stress, makes you feel happier, and gives you more energy. In fact, studies have shown that students who exercise regularly get better grades than those who don't.

Exercise doesn't have to mean joining a gym or running; it can be as simple as going for a walk. Here are some great ways to exercise:

- **Go for a walk or bike ride:** Even just a few minutes of physical activity can increase your heart rate and improve your mood.

- **Go to the park:** Going to the park with friends, kicking a ball around, or playing games is a great way to exercise while having fun.

- **Playing sports:** Playing sports like football, basketball, or baseball is a great way to get out and enjoy exercising in a team environment.

- **Swimming:** Swimming is one of the best all-body workout activities.

- **Dance:** Dancing increases your heart rate and is a great physical activity.

- **Walk, scoot, or cycle to school:** Incorporating your daily exercise into your journey to and from school is a great way to increase your daily physical activity.

With so many ways to exercise, you are sure to find something. The important thing is to find something you enjoy and make exercise a habit. And once you exercise regularly, you'll soon notice the mental and physical benefits.

Here are some tips to help you make exercise part of your everyday life:

- **Create a plan:** Make a plan and try to do at least 20 minutes of exercise every day.

- **Walk or ride your bicycle:** Instead of driving, try walking to school, cycling to friends, or scooting to the shops.

- **Join a gym or sports club:** Joining a gym and exercising with friends can be a fun way to stay active.

- **Encourage your friends to join you:** Exercising with friends is fun and adds extra motivation.

- **Set exercise goals:** Challenge yourself or compete with friends to reach goals, such as walking over 10,000 steps or running a specific distance.

- **Mix it up:** Try different ways to stay active, from running, to dancing, to online exercises.

- **Use fitness apps:** If you need extra motivation to get started, use online exercise videos.

Make Sure You Get Enough Sleep

Sleep is essential for both your physical and mental health. When you sleep, your body heals and rejuvenates itself. This is especially important when you're younger; with so much going on in your life and so many changes in your body, your body needs time to rest and recover.

When you have a good night's sleep, you wake up with the energy and focus you need to tackle a new day.

Sleep can also affect your mental health both positively and negatively. If you don't get enough sleep or have a bad night's sleep, you may feel tired and irritable and find it difficult to concentrate. Whereas after a good night's sleep, you'll find you're in a better mood. So as you can see, sleep really is your secret superpower!

How much sleep do you need?

The American Academy of Sleep Medicine recommends children aged 6 to 12 get 9–12 hours of sleep and teenagers 8–10 hours of sleep per night.

Here are some tips on how you can get the sleep you need to be at your best:

- **Create a relaxing bedtime routine:** This might include reading, meditating, taking a warm bath, or any other relaxing activity.

- **Avoid viewing computer and phone screens for at least an hour before bedtime:** The blue light from screens can interfere with sleep.

- **Cut down on caffeine and sugar during the afternoon and evening:** Caffeine and sugar are both stimulants and can make it hard to fall asleep.

- **Stick to a consistent sleep schedule:** Try to get up and go to bed at the same time every day, even on the weekends.

HOW TO GET
THE SLEEP YOU NEED TO BE AT YOUR BEST

1 Create a relaxing bedtime routine. This might include reading, meditation, or taking a warm bath.

2 Avoid viewing computer and phone screens for at least one hour before bedtime. The blue light from screens can interfere with your sleep.

3 Cut down on caffeine and sugar during the afternoon and evening.

4 Stick to a consistent sleep schedule. Try to get up and go to bed at the same time every day, even on the weekends.

If you take time to develop these physical self-care habits, it will help you feel better, prevent illnesses, and keep your body strong and healthy!

SECTION 3: HOW TO LOOK AFTER YOUR MENTAL AND EMOTIONAL HEALTH

Middle school can be challenging, and taking care of your mental and emotional well-being is as important as physical self-care.

Relax and Do Things You Enjoy

One way to care for your mental and emotional needs is to relax and do things you enjoy. Try to set aside some time daily to do something for you.

This could include:

SELF-CARE
Things you can do for self-care

Reading a book

Art projects

Taking a walk

Listening to music

Meditation

Spending time with your pet

Yoga

Doing anything else that helps you relax

Having time to do the things you enjoy and that make you happy gives you a break from the responsibilities of life.

Be Careful of Social Media

Social media is a wonderful thing. It's a great way to stay in touch with friends and family. It can be a great source of information and can be highly entertaining. But it can also be unhealthy. What you see on social media isn't always a true reflection of reality. People like to portray a perfect life on social media. The perfect car, the ideal body, the perfect relationship. But it's important to remember that what you see on social media is only a snapshot of someone's life and isn't always true.

So be careful comparing yourself or your life to what you see on social media. Remember that everyone is unique, special and has their own strengths and weaknesses.

Talk About Your Feelings

The feelings you have today are perfectly normal. In fact, the chances are someone else is feeling exactly the same way as you do. That's why it's essential to talk about them. Tell someone about it if you find something challenging or you don't feel right. Talking about how you feel to a parent, friend, or trusted adult can help you understand your feelings and devise ways to deal with them. Remember that it's always okay to reach out for help. As they say: "a problem shared, is a problem halved."

Be Kind to Yourself

School can be challenging, and you will likely make some mistakes along the way. But remember that everyone makes mistakes, so don't be too hard on yourself. Instead, stay positive, learn from your mistakes, and be kind to yourself.

SECTION 4: SOCIAL SELF-CARE – FRIENDS AND RELATIONSHIPS

Social self-care means that you take care of yourself when it comes to your relationships with the people around you. In other words, you pay attention to your own social needs.

One way to do this is to surround yourself with supportive people who help you feel good about yourself. When you have friends who help you feel happy and like to do the same things as you, it enables you to stay positive, maintain a growth mindset, and succeed in life.

However, not all friendships are healthy and positive. If people in your friendship circle make you feel bad about yourself, say mean things about others, or are constantly being negative, you do not have to continue spending time with them. That is where the boundary skills you learned earlier in this book come in.

Sometimes, you might feel that having a successful middle school social life means you should try to make friends with popular or cool students. But it is much better to have true friends who have similar interests and accept you for who you are.

How to Deal with Peer Pressure

In middle school, you may feel pressure to do things you aren't comfortable doing. This is called peer pressure, and it's common among teenagers. Sometimes peer pressure can be good, like when your friends encourage you to do something that challenges you and pushes you outside your comfort zone. But other times, peer pressure can make you feel like you have to do things you aren't comfortable with, like lying, cheating, or doing something dangerous.

Here are some tips to help you navigate peer pressure:

- **Say "no":** When you feel pressured to do something you aren't comfortable with or believe is wrong, just say "no." Sticking to your principles and saying "no" shows that you have boundaries and you aren't willing to cross them.

- **Use "I" statements:** When dealing with peer pressure, try to use "I" statements. *For example, saying, "That is not something I want to do," is a more robust response than "That is a silly idea."*

- **Be different:** Peer pressure is all about feeling like you have to fit in. But it's okay to be different. And it's okay to say "no." Remember, you are fantastic, just as you are.

- **Choose your friends:** If you feel constant pressure to do things you're not comfortable with, then perhaps it's time to look for some new friends. Surround yourself with people who respect you and like you for who you are.

- **Seek help from a trusted adult:** If you're facing a difficult situation, talk to a parent, teacher, counselor, or trusted adult. They can support and guide you through the problem you're trying to navigate.

How to Deal with Bullying

Unfortunately, bullying is an all too common occurrence at school. If you are a target of bullying, it can be very unpleasant and can affect your mental and physical health. Bullying comes in many forms, including name-calling, gossip, and online bullying.

Hopefully, you'll never be the target of bullies, but here are some ways to cope, just in case.

- **Bullying is NOT okay.** It goes without saying that bullying is not OK. Nobody should feel threatened or unsafe due to another's actions.

- **Don't ignore it.** If you are being bullied, don't ignore it. Speak to someone you trust who can help you solve the problem.

- **Stand up for yourself.** Bullies take advantage of people who are scared to stand up for themselves. If you can, try telling the bully calmly, confidently, and assertively that their actions and behavior are unacceptable.

- **Develop your "anti bully" armor.** Reacting to bullies with strength and confidence is the best way to tell them their actions won't hurt you. If you can "shrug off" comments rather than reacting angrily, you'll send a strong message to the bully.

- **Tell someone.** If you are being bullied and cannot resolve the situation, tell someone you trust, such as your teacher or parents. This might be difficult, but it is the most important thing you can do to resolve the situation.

Getting Involved in The Community to Improve Social Well-Being

Community involvement and volunteer work are great ways of getting yourself out into the community and learning more about the world you live in. No matter where you are, there are sure to be organizations that can use your help.

When you volunteer, you're doing something to positively impact your community. Many volunteer positions allow you to learn new skills or build on your existing skills. You will also have the opportunity to make new friends that have similar interests to your own. Volunteering also looks great on future college or job applications and can help boost self-confidence and mental health. It is excellent to know you did something that made a difference!

So, where can you volunteer?

Your school, community center, or local government office probably has a list of organizations with opportunities for middle schoolers to volunteer. Here are some ways that middle schoolers can help out:

- **Community cleanup projects:** Many areas have community clean-up projects where they need volunteers to clean up parks, rake leaves, paint benches, and plant flowers and trees.

- **Fundraising:** All organizations need funds for their projects. Perhaps you could volunteer to help with an existing fundraising project. You could also go to the organization director with ideas for how you and your friends can organize a fundraising event.

- **Animal shelters:** Many animal shelters depend heavily on the help of volunteers. If you love working with cats, dogs, or other animals, ask your local animal shelter if you can help walk dogs, clean cages, or spend time visiting with animals to help socialize them.

- **Tutoring and mentoring:** If you enjoy working with children, consider tutoring or mentoring. You can do this by offering to read to young children, helping them with their homework, or spending time with them as a role model.

- **Food banks and soup kitchens:** Nearly every community has at least one food bank or soup kitchen. They usually need help collecting and sorting food donations, passing them out to people, and fundraising.

- **Elder visits:** Some communities have programs where tweens and teens can visit with the elderly in nursing homes or senior centers. Depending on their needs, you can read to them, play games with them, or talk to them and keep them company.

- **Cultural events:** One way to volunteer and learn about other cultures simultaneously is to volunteer to help at a cultural festival in your area. These events usually need volunteers to help set up displays, hand out brochures, and do other tasks.

Volunteering can be rewarding and fun! The key is to find volunteer opportunities that match your interest and skills, then start doing what you can to help!

. . . .

SECTION 5: SPIRITUAL SELF-CARE

Spiritual self-care is any activity you do that nurtures your spirit. Although some people center their spiritual self-care around their religious beliefs, spiritual self-care does not have to be a religious activity. It can be anything you do to develop your sense of self in connection with your spiritual values.

Some great spiritual self-care practices for middle schoolers include:

- **Connecting with nature:** This can involve going for a walk or a hike or just sitting on a bench in a natural setting and relaxing. Listen to birds, flowing water, the wind, and other sounds surrounding you when you do this.

- **Journaling:** Writing can help you to explore your personal values and purpose. One type of journaling you might want to try is stream-of-consciousness journaling, where you write without pausing for a set period. This journaling can give you many important insights into your thought process.

- **Gratitude journaling:** Another way you can use your journal for spiritual self-care is through gratitude journaling. Take time each day to think about things you are grateful for and write them in your journal.

- **Meditation:** Meditating is a great way to calm your mind and connect with your inner thoughts. At first, it might be hard to focus on meditating for more than a few minutes. Still, if you meditate daily, you will soon find it easier to meditate for longer sessions.

- **Random acts of kindness:** Doing something kind for someone every day is another excellent way to connect with your spiritual side. It could be something as simple as holding the door open for someone or writing a note of encouragement to a friend or relative who needs it.

- **Religion:** Some people connect to their spirituality by participating in religious services at churches, synagogues, mosques, or other spiritual communities. Many of these organizations have youth groups and activities where you can explore your personal spirituality with like-minded people.

Remember, spiritual self-care is unique to each individual, and finding what works for you is essential. Explore different practices to see which ones you find the most helpful. Once you find spiritual self-care activities you enjoy, do them regularly. You'll soon see the benefits of doing things that nurture your spirit!

SECTION 6: PUTTING IT INTO PRACTICE

Now that you know how important self-care is, here are some tips to help you get started. Remember, self-care doesn't need to be complicated and time-consuming. It can be as simple as taking a walk, reading a book, or taking a few minutes to meditate.

- **Eat healthy:** Replace sugary or salty snacks with healthy foods you enjoy.

- **Be active:** Add exercise to your weekly schedule.

- **Unplug and disconnect:** Turn off your computer and other electronic devices an hour before bedtime.

- **Be careful comparing yourself to others:** Remember, what you see on social media is only a snapshot of someone's life and isn't always true.

- **Say "no":** Stick to your principles, and don't be afraid to say "no" if you're uncomfortable doing something.

- **Bullying is NOT okay:** Tell someone if you are being bullied.

- **Do things you love:** Make time in your schedule for enjoyable and relaxing activities.

- **Volunteer:** Look for opportunities to volunteer in your community.

- **Diversify:** Try at least one new spiritual self-care activity each week.

Adopting the strategies above can protect and improve your well-being, which will help you succeed in middle school and beyond.

NATURE QUEST

Boost your spirit and reconnect with nature using this fun and easy checklist!

☐ Take a walk in a local park or forest.

☐ Plant and care for a small garden or houseplant.

☐ Draw or paint a landscape or a nature object that you find interesting or beautiful.

☐ Watch the sunrise or set over the horizon.

Spend some time near the water. ☐

☐ Sit quietly outside and listen to the sounds of nature.

Enjoy a picnic in a natural setting. ☐

☐ Go for a bike ride in a natural area.

☐ Lie down on the grass and look at the clouds. What shapes can you see?

CHAPTER 8:

RESPONSIBILITY AND OWNERSHIP

"It is only when you take responsibility for your life that you discover how powerful you truly are."
– Allanah Hunt, author and life coach.

Responsibility is a vital success skill for middle schoolers to develop. Being responsible enables you to make good choices, take ownership of your actions, and build a solid foundation of trust with others.

You already have responsibilities at school, home, and community. As you enter high school and college and become an adult, the number and type of responsibilities you have will increase.

In this chapter, we'll explore what responsibility means, why it's essential, and how you can develop a better sense of responsibility. We'll also provide strategies for practicing responsibility in different areas of your life.

Topics we'll explore in this chapter include:

- Understanding responsibility
- Responsibility at school
- Responsibility at home
- Responsibility in the community
- Managing the consequences

Ready? Let's get started!

SECTION 1: UNDERSTANDING RESPONSIBILITY

First off, what is responsibility?

Responsibility is being dependable, trustworthy, organized, on time, and accountable for your words and actions.

We often think of responsibilities as tasks we are expected to perform, such as doing homework, feeding a pet, taking out the trash, or cutting the lawn. But responsibilities extend beyond doing specific jobs to the actions we take every day, including how we behave and interact with the world around us.

As you get older, your responsibilities grow. You are expected to take on more ownership of your life, decisions, and what you say and do. And if things go wrong, you have the skills to be accountable for your actions and do what you can to make amends.

More Responsibility = More Freedom

There are many benefits of being responsible. How you deal with responsibilities is essential to your character and reputation. When you are known for acting responsibly, you will gain the trust and respect of your parents, teachers, classmates, and everyone you know.

When your parents and other adults see that you are becoming more responsible, they'll realize you are ready to take on new responsibilities that will give you greater freedom and help you learn and grow.

The Importance of Accountability

Some people confuse the meaning of responsibility and accountability. Responsibility is about completing tasks, keeping promises, and acting and speaking responsibly. Accountability, on the other hand, is about owning up to and accepting the consequences of your actions.

> *For example, if you arrive late to school, it's your responsibility to tell the teacher and ensure it doesn't happen again. But accountability means you take ownership of coming late, recognizing that it was your fault. And you take responsibility and accept any possible consequences for being late, such as a detention or apologizing to your teacher.*

Accountability is an integral part of being a responsible person. It means you're willing to own up to the consequences of your actions.

SECTION 2: HOW TO TAKE CHARGE OF YOUR LEARNING

As a middle schooler, it's your responsibility to make the most of your education. This means being organized, managing time, and developing good study habits. It's all about taking ownership of your learning and making it your own. But what does that mean exactly?

When you take charge of your learning, you become the boss of your education. You understand that you—not your parents, the school, or your teachers—are responsible for what you learn and how well you do at school.

Another way to consider it is to think of your learning as a journey. It's up to you to determine where you want to go and how you will get there.

Here are some ways to take charge of your learning journey:

● Develop good study habits.
● Set goals for yourself, such as improving your grades or taking challenging new classes.
● Participate in discussions and projects.
● Ask questions if you need more information.
● Be curious and look for opportunities to learn more about the subjects that interest you.
● Go above and beyond the minimum requirements for assignments and projects.
● Own up and take full responsibility for your mistakes.

And here are some tips on how to show responsibility at school:

- **Be prepared:** Hand in your homework on time and bring the stuff you need for class.

- **Pay attention:** Listen to your teacher and pay attention in class.

- **Turn off your phone:** If you bring a phone to school, set it on silent.

- **Participate in class discussions:** Put your hand up and be heard in class.

- **Ask questions:** If something needs to be clarified, ask your teacher.

- **Show respect:** Always treat your teachers and classmates with respect and kindness.

Remember, taking charge of your learning journey involves owning your decisions and recognizing that you can shape your future success. You've got this!

SECTION 3: HOW TO BE RESPONSIBLE AT HOME

School is not the only place where you have responsibilities. Your home is another important place to learn and take responsibility for your actions and behavior.

At home, your responsibilities include helping out around the house, setting the table, taking care of pets, cleaning your room, looking after younger brothers and sisters, or helping clean the house. You also have responsibilities to your family, like listening to each other, respecting their opinions, spending quality time together, or discussing how you are getting on at school.

When you and everyone in your family know their responsibilities, life becomes smoother and happier.

Here are some ways to take responsibility at home:

- **Create a daily routine:** Write your chores in your planner or schedule. That way, you'll be less likely to forget them.

- **Do your chores:** Don't wait until someone has to remind you. Get it done immediately, and you won't have to worry about it later.

- **Tidy your stuff:** This includes clothes, sports equipment, books, and other things that must be put away.

- **Be respectful:** Listen to your parents or other family members and respect their wishes.

- **Apologize:** We all make mistakes. If you forget to do a chore or misbehave, take ownership and apologize for your actions.

And when you do chores around the house, treat them as a learning opportunity. Mowing the lawn, setting the table, washing the car, or taking out the trash are all skills you'll need when you're older and have your own place.

Being Part of the Family Team

Your responsibilities at home aren't just about chores. You are also responsible for being a part of the family team.

This might mean offering to help with extra tasks, helping your brothers or sisters with their school work, or joining in with family games and activities. These activities are great ways to strengthen your family bond and have fun together!

Some ways to build your family team include:

- Preparing meals
- Planning a family picnic
- Volunteering together
- Planning a vacation together
- Making and burying a family time capsule
- Researching your family tree
- Playing board games together
- Watching a TV show or movie together
- Going to fairs, concerts, and other events as a family
- Camping together
- Cleaning up the house or yard together

Being Kind and Considerate at Home

Part of being a responsible family member is being considerate of the other people in the household. This means respecting each other's space, privacy, property, and opinions.

> *For example, keep the noise down if one of your brothers or sisters is trying to study. If you want to listen to loud music, use headphones.*

Respect and consideration also involve the language that you use. Suppose everyone in the family uses kind and considerate language. In that case, it will help keep communication open and make the home nicer.

SECTION 4: HOW TO BE A RESPONSIBLE NEIGHBOR

You might not realize it, but as a middle schooler, there's a lot you can do to help out in your neighborhood and community. Helping out in the community not only helps those living there, but it's also about being a good citizen when you grow up.

Ways you can help out in your community include:

- Volunteering with community organizations
- Cleaning up parks and walkways
- Planting flowers
- Recycling
- Helping elderly neighbors with yard work and other chores
- Helping at community events
- Learning about issues that affect your community
- Following the rules in your community

Community involvement is also a great way to meet and build new relationships with adults, tweens, and teens in your area. In addition, many community projects, especially those run by organizations, require teamwork, which is a great way to learn essential life skills like communication, collaboration, and problem-solving.

By getting involved in your community, you'll have the chance to make it a better place for everyone to live now and into the future! So go out there and get involved! You'll be glad you did.

SECTION 5: HOW TO HANDLE MISTAKES

No matter how hard we try, everyone makes mistakes. Taking ownership of and learning from your mistakes is integral to personal growth and development.

Here's what you can do when you make a mistake:

- **Admit it:** Even though it can be embarrassing, confessing to a mistake is better than having someone else discover it later.

- **Own it:** Let everyone affected by your mistake know that you take full responsibility and that you will not try to blame others or make excuses.

- **Apologize:** Say sorry to those affected by your mistake, and try to make things right.

- **Learn from it:** Consider what went wrong and what you could have done differently. This will help you avoid making similar mistakes again in the future.

Accepting the Consequences of Mistakes

Sometimes, you will make small mistakes, like putting your shoes on the wrong feet when you're in a hurry. But other times, your mistakes might cause problems that affect others, such as damaging property, forgetting something important, or making poor decisions.

You should expect to deal with the consequences when you make these mistakes. Sometimes, the consequence will be imposed by a teacher, parent, or other person affected by your mistake.

For example, suppose you break your neighbor's flowerpot while playing ball. In that case, you might have to clean up the mess and use your allowance to replace the flowerpot. Or if you forget to close the door and the dog runs away, you might miss out on time with your friends to search for your dog.

As a responsible person, it is important to accept that actions, however small, have consequences. Taking responsibility for your actions and mistakes is one of the toughest but essential things you can do. It will help you to build character and learn important lessons.

Learning to Forgive Yourself

It's normal to feel bad when you make a mistake and have to deal with the consequences. You might feel you've let yourself down. You might feel like you've let other people down. But if you've owned up to the mistake and faced the consequences of your actions, try to learn from it and move on.

Remember, we all make mistakes; the key is learning from them.

SECTION 6: PUTTING IT INTO PRACTICE

Now that you understand the importance of taking responsibility, it's time to start practicing what you've learned. Here are some tips to get you started:

- **Develop good study habits:** Set goals for yourself, participate in discussions, ask questions, and look for opportunities to learn more about subjects that interest you.

- **Do your chores:** Create a checklist of your home responsibilities, do your chores without being reminded, and tidy your stuff away.

- **Be part of the family team:** Get involved in preparing meals, help with extra tasks, and join in with family activities.

- **Learn from mistakes:** Own your mistakes, apologize, and make things right.

- **Don't feel too bad:** Remember, we all make mistakes. Don't be too hard on yourself. Learn from them and move on.

By adopting the strategies above and in the chapter, you'll be able to take on more responsibility as you progress through middle school and beyond.

MY RESPONSIBILITIES

List down your tasks at home, commitments to yourself, school duties, and ways you contribute to your community.

1 TO MYSELF

- ○
- ○
- ○
- ○
- ○
- ○
- ○
- ○
- ○
- ○
- ○
- ○
- ○

2 AT HOME

- ○
- ○
- ○
- ○
- ○
- ○
- ○
- ○
- ○
- ○
- ○
- ○
- ○

3 AT SCHOOL

- ○
- ○
- ○
- ○
- ○
- ○
- ○
- ○
- ○
- ○
- ○
- ○
- ○

4 IN THE COMMUNITY

- ○
- ○
- ○
- ○
- ○
- ○
- ○
- ○
- ○
- ○
- ○
- ○
- ○

CHAPTER 9:

SETTING GOALS AND REACHING THEM

"You can, you should, and, if you're brave enough to start, you will."
— Stephen King, author.

Goal setting is a crucial life skill. Learning to set a goal and make a workable plan is the surest path to success in life. In this chapter, we will explore the benefits of goal setting, provide strategies for setting and achieving goals, and discuss how to overcome possible obstacles.

Topics we'll cover in this chapter include:

● Understanding goals
● How to set SMART goals
● Staying motivated
● Dealing with setbacks

Are you ready? Let's start learning to set goals that will help you achieve your dreams!

SECTION 1: UNDERSTANDING GOALS

As a middle schooler, you probably have many things you want to achieve. Maybe it's earning enough money to go to a concert, making the school soccer team, finishing school projects on time, improving your grades, or making new friends. These are all examples of goals that are essential for success in every area of life.

Let's look at why goals are so important, the different types of goals, and why it helps to write down and track your goals.

Different Types of Goals

Just as there are many things you want to achieve in life, there are different kinds of goals. Some goals are personal, while others have to do with your success in school. Most goals can be categorized as long-term or short-term.

- **Short-term goals** can be achieved in days, weeks, or months, like completing a school project, planning a camping trip, reading a book, or trying out for the school swim team. Some short-term goals are stepping stones into longer-term goals.

- **Long-term goals** take a lot of planning and can take several months, a year, or more to achieve. Long-term goals include graduating from college, becoming a professional musician, or publishing a book.

It is good to have a mix of short-term and long-term goals. Short-term goals build confidence and motivation and can help you achieve your longer-term goals.

WHY GOALS MATTER

Goals are like your guiding light. They help you figure out where you want to go and how to get there. Here's why they are essential:

FOCUS AND MOTIVATION

When you know what your goals are and why you want to achieve them—and have an action plan to accomplish them—you will be more likely to put in the time and effort it takes to make them happen.

DIRECTION AND PURPOSE

Goals help you prioritize your time. For example, if your goal is to finish a school project on time, that becomes your priority until it is finished. It also means putting off watching that new TV show until after the project is done.

CONFIDENCE

Hitting goals builds your confidence. The more goals you accomplish, the more confidence you'll have to set bigger and more challenging goals in the future.

Writing Down and Tracking Your Goals

Whether working towards long- or short-term goals, writing down your goals and tracking your progress is a great way to stay on track. Here are two reasons why:

● **Motivation:** Seeing what you've already done and the actions you plan to take toward achieving your goals in the future helps you stay motivated.

● **Focus:** Writing down your goals helps you to maintain a clear vision of what you want to accomplish and why.

● **Back-up:** Sometimes, things happen beyond your control. Maybe a storm knocks out your power, or your Wi-Fi goes down. If you have your goals written down, you can have a record of where you left off and what you need to do next.

In short, writing down your goals and tracking your progress is an effective way to achieve success in all areas of life.

• •

SECTION 2: HOW TO SET SMART GOALS

When setting goals, it's helpful to use the SMART goal method.

SMART goal setting is a method that makes goals clear and reachable. It was developed to help business owners with practical goal setting, but it works just as well for students.

For a goal to be SMART, it must be Specific, Measurable, Achievable, Relevant, and Time-bound. Let's look at the elements of a SMART goal:

● **Specific.** This means your goal should be clear. The more precise the goal, the more likely you are to achieve it. *For example, "I want* to improve my math grades from a C to A B this semester" instead of "I want to improve my maths grade."

- **Measurable.** The success of your goal should be measurable. For example, if your goal is to get better grades, you can track your progress against the goals you achieve.

- **Achievable.** This means your goal should be something you can reasonably expect to achieve. *For example, learning the basics of playing football during the summer to make the middle school football team is an achievable goal. Being drafted into the NFL after playing one season of middle school football is not.*

- **Relevant.** Achieving a goal takes hard work and dedication. That's why goals should be appropriate and matter to you. *For example, a relevant goal for an art student might be to get their paintings displayed in a gallery.*

- **Time-bound.** A goal should be accomplished within a specific time. *For example, "I will complete my science project two days before the school science fair."*

Of course, setting goals is the first step; staying motivated and on track is how you reach the destination, as you'll soon see.

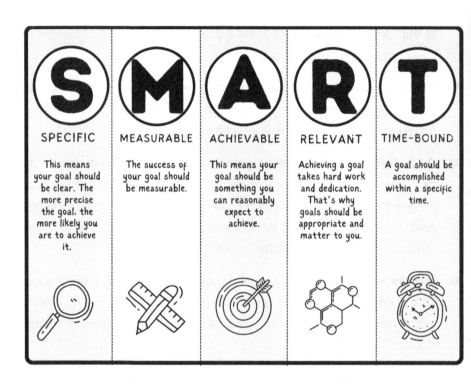

SPECIFIC	MEASURABLE	ACHIEVABLE	RELEVANT	TIME-BOUND
This means your goal should be clear. The more precise the goal, the more likely you are to achieve it.	The success of your goal should be measurable.	This means your goal should be something you can reasonably expect to achieve.	Achieving a goal takes hard work and dedication. That's why goals should be appropriate and matter to you.	A goal should be accomplished within a specific time.

SECTION 3: HOW TO STAY MOTIVATED

Setting a goal is like learning to play a musical instrument. At first, it's new and exciting, and you can't wait to practice. But when things get more demanding, and your progress slows, it becomes more difficult to motivate yourself. This is when it can be tempting to forget about your dream to become a musician, give up and find something else to do.

So how do you keep on going? How can you avoid giving up? How can you persevere to achieve your dreams?

Here are some tips to help you stay motivated:

- **Visualize success:** When you feel your motivation slipping, picture yourself reaching your goal. Imagine how you will feel. Then imagine how awesome it will be to tell your friends, family, and teachers about your success.

- **Share your goals:** Tell your friends and family about your goals and dreams. Sharing them with your loved ones makes them real and can act as a great motivator.

- **Celebrate victories:** Take some time to celebrate small wins along the way. Even though the journey to achieving your goal may take months or even years, there are many small victories you can celebrate along the way. Celebrating these steps will help you stay motivated and confident.

Dealing with Setbacks

Everyone who sets out to achieve something faces setbacks and obstacles. The key is to stay resilient and not let setbacks discourage you. Remember that setbacks are just part of the journey. You can learn from them, like the famous inventors Alexander Graham Bell, Thomas Edison, and Steve Jobs. Their inventions changed the world, but only after they faced and overcame obstacles.

So remember, whatever setbacks you face, if you have a goal, keep going. You can do anything you set your mind to.

SECTION 4: PUTTING IT INTO PRACTICE

Now that you know more about goal setting and why it is crucial, here are some strategies you can adopt to keep making progress toward your goals:

- **Set SMART goals:** Use the SMART goal method to set your goals. Ensure they are Specific, Measurable, Achievable, Relevant, and Time-bound.

- **Share your goals:** Tell your friends and family about your plans.

- **Visualize success:** If you feel your motivation slipping. Picture yourself reaching your goals.

- **Celebrate wins:** Break big goals into smaller chunks and celebrate each victory as you achieve them.

- **Overcome setbacks:** We all face setbacks along the way. Do not let them discourage you; remember, they are just part of the journey.

By adopting the tips above and in this chapter, you can be sure you'll be able to set and achieve your goals in no time!

LET'S SET A
SMART GOAL

What's something you really want to achieve this school year? Make it Specific, Measurable, Achievable, Relevant, and Time-bound.

S | SPECIFIC |

M | MEASURABLE |

A | ACHIEVABLE |

R | RELEVANT |

T | TIME-BOUND |

CHAPTER 10:

HIGH SCHOOL: YOUR NEXT BIG ADVENTURE

"Education is the key to unlocking the world, a passport to freedom."
– Oprah Winfrey, TV host.

As you approach the end of middle school, you might be wondering, "What's high school going to be like?"

Moving from middle to high school can feel like going from a playground to an amusement park—exciting but slightly daunting!

You might have questions like, "Can I keep up with the classes and homework?" "Will I be able to make new friends?" "Which clubs should I join?"

Don't worry! In this chapter, we will explore how you can prepare for high school and college and your future career.

Topics covered in this chapter include:

● Academic preparation

- Extracurricular activities
- The big step to high school
- Being yourself and embracing your individuality
- Career choices
- Mentors and support systems

Ready? Let's get started!

· ·

SECTION 1: HOW TO STUDY SMART

The work you put in at middle school lays the groundwork for what you will learn in high school. Put another way, if high school is the skyscraper of knowledge, middle school is where you build the foundations. The stronger the foundations, the higher you can build.

Here are some tips on how to study smart:

- **Plan your time:** Create a study schedule that guides you on what to do and when.

- **Learn the material:** Instead of memorizing facts, try to understand the lessons and concepts.

- **Be an active learner:** Be curious, ask questions in class, and go the extra mile with your homework. Do whatever it takes to get involved.

- **Ask for help:** If you're having trouble understanding something, ask your teacher for help.

Doing Your Best in Exams

Exams can be daunting. For some students, they are a source of anxiety and stress, while for others, they are an opportunity to show what they know. Whatever your attitude to exams, one thing remains true for everyone—the best way to do well is to prepare and practice. The more you do them, the better you'll become.

Here are some tips for excelling in exams:

How to Prepare for Exams

- **Start early:** Start studying for exams well in advance. This will give you plenty of time to make sure you understand the material.

- **Know the topics:** Ensure you know what material you will be tested on.

- **Study regularly:** Don't wait until the night before to start studying. You will retain more from regular study than trying to cram the night before the exam.

- **Prepare with test papers:** Ask your teacher if the exam will be multiple choice, short answers, essay, etc. Then take practice test papers to identify and improve any weak areas.

- **Make a study plan:** If you have several exams to prepare for, it's a good idea to break down each subject into topics and allocate time for studying them.

- **Use flashcards:** Besides reading the material, quiz yourself with flashcards, record it and listen to it, or ask friends and family to test you.

- **Look after yourself:** Preparing for exams can sometimes be stressful. Remember to look after your own health: get plenty of sleep, take regular breaks, eat healthily, and get regular exercise.

Once the exam day is finally here, it's time to show what you know. Here are some tips to excel on exam day:

How to Excel on Exam Day

- **Fuel your body and mind:** Do your best to eat healthy food, drink plenty of water, and get enough sleep before taking a test. This will help you to feel positive and focused.

- **Arrive early:** Allow plenty of time to get to the classroom or exam hall so that you arrive relaxed and not rushed.

- **Read the questions carefully:** Read the questions carefully, and ensure you understand what they are asking before answering them.

- **Manage your time:** If unsure of a question, try not to dwell on it too long. Move on, answer the questions you are confident of, and return to it later.

- **Review your answers:** If you have time at the end of the test, review your answers and check your work for any obvious mistakes.

If you follow the tips above, you can approach exams as an opportunity to show your knowledge and tackle them with confidence.

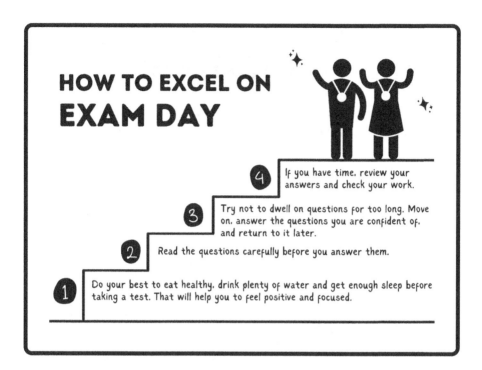

HOW TO EXCEL ON EXAM DAY

4 If you have time, review your answers and check your work.

3 Try not to dwell on questions for too long. Move on, answer the questions you are confident of, and return to it later.

2 Read the questions carefully before you answer them.

1 Do your best to eat healthy, drink plenty of water and get enough sleep before taking a test. That will help you to feel positive and focused.

SECTION 2: HOW TO GET INVOLVED IN AFTER-SCHOOL ACTIVITIES

Extracurricular activities are essential to school life. They allow you to develop skills outside the classroom and pursue your interests and passions. They're also a great place to meet friends who share similar interests. Plus, they give your application a real boost when applying to colleges!

But with so many activities to choose from, it can sometimes be challenging to decide on the ones to pick. The key is to pick activities that you're interested in, and that match your future goals.

AFTER-SCHOOL ACTIVITIES

Once you reach high school, you'll have even more activities to choose from. While they will vary from school to school, here are some of the more common ones:

SPORTS

Including football, soccer, basketball, track, tennis and swimming.

MUSIC

Including band, choir, and orchestra.

JOURNALISM

Students that are interested in writing and publishing often sign up to help with the school newspaper or magazine.

DRAMA

School theater programs offer students the opportunity to act, direct, design stage sets, and costumes.

COMMUNITY SERVICE ORGANIZATIONS

Programs that give students the opportunity to volunteer in their community.

VISUAL ARTS

Includes drawing, painting, photography, sculpturing, etc.

CLUBS

Some popular clubs include chess, robotics, debate, environment, foreign language, civil rights, academic and computer clubs.

Once you reach high school, you'll have even more activities to choose from. While they vary from school to school, here are some more common ones:

- **Sports:** Popular high school sports include football, soccer, basketball, track, tennis, and swimming.

- **Music:** Music programs, including band, choir, and orchestra.

- **Drama:** School theater programs allow students to act, direct, design stage sets, and design costumes.

- **Community service organizations:** Many high schools have programs that allow students to volunteer in their communities.

- **Clubs:** Most high schools have a wide selection of clubs students can join, such as chess, robotics, debate, environment, foreign language, civil rights, academic, and computer clubs.

- **Journalism:** If writing is your passion, consider joining the school newspaper or magazine. It's a great way to dip your toes into the world of journalism.

- **Visual arts:** This category includes drawing, painting, photography, or sculpturing.

SECTION 3: HOW TO MAKE THE BIG STEP TO HIGH SCHOOL

The transition from middle to high school can feel like a huge step. But remember, this time, you're prepared. You've already successfully navigated the step from elementary to middle school. And equipped with your superstar skills, a positive attitude, and a growth mindset, you're more than ready to face the challenges of high school.

HIGH SCHOOL:
MYTHS & FACTS

As a middle school student, you have probably heard many things about high school already. Unfortunately, not everything you hear or see is true. Let's clarify some myths about high school life and give you the facts.

MYTHS VS	FACTS
"As long as I have good grades, there's no need to get involved in extracurricular activities."	While good grades are important, high school is more than academic success. It's a great place to explore your interests. Most colleges will look favorably on students who actively pursue their passions. Plus, it's great fun, and you'll meet some interesting people.
"Only popular kids and star athletes have a positive experience at high school."	While this is the image many movies and TV shows portray, it isn't true. Just as with middle school, there are many different individuals at high school, all with unique talents. You don't have to be a sports star to have a good time; you just need to be yourself. Then find your group of friends that like you for who you are.
"High school years are the best years of your life."	High school is a different experience for every student. Some people find the high school experience more straightforward to navigate than others. While some students thrive, others have a more challenging time. But, many students who find high school difficult go on to have positive experiences in college and in their careers after graduation. The key is that every student's journey is different.

Being Yourself and Embracing Your Individuality

You might have heard people say: "just be yourself." While this sounds simple, what exactly does it mean? Who else could you be?

In middle and high school, some students feel pressure to try to fit in by following the crowd and copying others.

But it's important to remember that each of us is unique and wonderfully special. We all have different personalities, interests, and skills. So embrace your individuality, be proud of who you are, and don't be afraid to stand out. Being yourself is the greatest gift you can give yourself, ultimately leading to a happier, more fulfilling life.

Here are some tips for being yourself in middle school and high school:

- **Figure out what you enjoy:** Take time to think about things you enjoy and what you are good at. This can be music, art, sports, writing, animal care, or anything! These are the things that make you unique.

- **Find good, supportive friends:** Do your best to make friends with encouraging people who have a positive attitude and accept you for who you are.

- **Be proud of who you are:** Whether you dress differently, have a different hairstyle, enjoy different activities, or listen to different music, be proud of who you are and what you enjoy!

- **Explore your interests:** Don't be afraid to pursue what you enjoy, even if it differs from most people you know. Not everyone is into the same things. Maybe you like listening to heavy metal, and your best friend loves opera. Chances are you have many other interests you can have fun talking about.

- **Remember that everyone is different in their own way:** Even students who seem to follow the crowd in everything they do have unique perspectives.

If you do these things, it will help you feel confident and happy being yourself as you navigate your way through middle school, high school, and beyond.

. . . .

SECTION 4: HOW TO NETWORK AND CHOOSE A CAREER

At this stage, you might already have some ideas about what career might interest you.

Perhaps it's influenced by the adults close to you, like your family or neighbors. Or maybe you're drawn to the subjects you do well in at school. Whatever the case, career choices are not something you have to decide now. But both middle and high school are good places to start exploring different career paths.

Some ways of learning about career possibilities include:

- **Networking:** Talk to adults about their jobs and ask what they like and dislike about them.

- **Researching:** Search online resources, speak to teachers, and learn about the different careers available to you.

- **Attending events:** Take advantage of school career days by listening to speakers from different professions.

- **Stay up to date with technological developments:** With the emergence of new technology, new types of jobs are constantly being created. By the time you finish high school or college, you might find the perfect career for you is a job that doesn't even exist today!

When you are thinking about career choices, the important thing to remember is to follow your passions, keep your options open, continue learning, and stay positive!

SECTION 5: MENTORS AND SUPPORT SYSTEMS

Good mentors and a dependable support system become increasingly important as you navigate high school and college. Their guidance and encouragement are essential when you need advice, help with decisions, or someone to talk to when you're struggling.

Here are some tips for finding and cultivating relationships with mentors and support systems:

- **Identify your role models:** They could be counselors, teachers, coaches, relatives, or students you admire. Learn how they deal with opportunities, challenges, and setbacks.

- **Seek Teacher's Guidance:** Teachers can be an excellent source of help. They know you and what you are capable of and are in a perfect position to help you reach your goals.

- **Develop a strong network of friends:** A strong network can offer support and encouragement when you most need it.

- **Lean on guidance counselors:** School guidance counselors are experts in helping students with academic problems, emotional and social issues, and career guidance.

- **Talk to your parents:** Even if they don't have all the answers, they can help you connect with people, organizations, and resources to answer your questions.

Networking

Middle and high school are the ideal time to learn how to network and build relationships to help you learn, expand, and reach your goals. Knowing how to network is valuable in your personal and professional development.

So, what exactly is networking?

Networking involves interacting to exchange information and develop social or professional contacts.

Networking is all about building positive relationships. It can also open the doors to opportunities you may not otherwise know about. *For example, many people use networking to learn about scholarships, internships, job openings, and volunteer work.* Just keep in mind that networking is a two-way street: it's important to always be willing to help others in return for the help and advice they give you.

There are many ways to network. They include:
- Connections you make on social media
- Extracurricular activity friends, teachers, and coaches
- School career day presenters
- Organizations you volunteer with

● Clubs and groups outside of school

Starting to develop your network now or when you're in high school can help you learn about potential career paths and open up opportunities throughout your life.

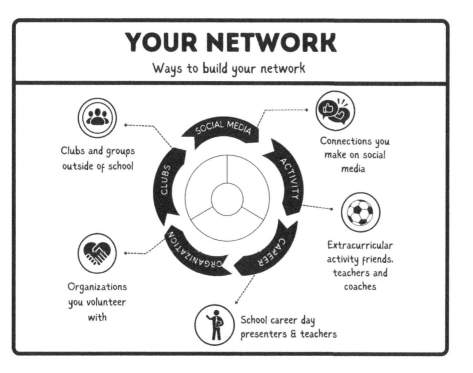

YOUR NETWORK
Ways to build your network

Clubs and groups outside of school

SOCIAL MEDIA

CLUBS

ACTIVITY

CAREER

ORGANIZATION

Connections you make on social media

Extracurricular activity friends, teachers and coaches

Organizations you volunteer with

School career day presenters & teachers

SECTION 6: PUTTING IT INTO PRACTICE

Now that you have a better idea of what to expect when you enter high school, here are some tips that can help you be ready to have a great high school experience:

● **Study smart:** Plan your time, understand and learn the material, be an active learner, and don't hesitate to ask for help.

- **Prepare for exams:** Don't wait until the last minute; prepare early, use test papers, and create a study plan.

- **Excel on exam day:** Fuel your body and mind, arrive early, read the questions carefully, answer what you can, and don't panic. You've got this!

- **Embrace your individuality:** You are unique, and you don't have to try to be someone else. Be proud of who you are.

- **Build your team:** As you navigate high school, your support system will become increasingly important. Identify role models and develop a strong network of friends.

By following these strategies and tips, you will be able to successfully navigate the step up from middle school to high school.

MY NEXT CHAPTER

Write about your hopes, dreams, and the steps you plan to take in your next adventure:

CHAPTER 11:

LOOKING FORWARD

The middle school years are a journey. And just like any journey, they're filled with opportunities, adventures, and challenges.

In middle school, you will make new friends, learn about exciting new subjects, explore different ideas, and discover new passions. It's a time of growth and self-discovery, where you'll learn much about yourself.

During this journey, you'll meet new people and form long-lasting friendships. Some of the friendships you make will last a lifetime. You'll meet people from different backgrounds with different interests. Through these new relationships, you'll improve your social skills and see the world from different perspectives.

But just like any adventure, you'll also face some challenges. You'll be juggling more work, after-school activities, and friendship groups. You'll be expected to take on more responsibility and decision-making. In short, your parents, friends, and teachers will expect more of you. And you might not always get it right the first time.

But that's okay. Remember that every challenge, every mistake, and every lesson learned is a stepping stone on your journey toward becoming an independent, successful, and confident adult. And you're not alone on this journey. You have a support network of family, teachers, and friends who are ready and willing to help you when times get tough or if you just need encouragement.

And finally, as you sail through middle school into high school, remember to enjoy every moment and every experience. Middle school isn't just about getting good grades or excelling in sports; it's about enjoying yourself and creating memories.

So go out there, create memories, find your tribe, achieve something incredible, and most importantly, be yourself.

Good luck,

Your friend
Ferne Bowe

THANKS
FOR READING OUR
BOOK!

We hope it has been helpful in teaching your teen important success skills that will serve them well throughout their life.

We would be so grateful if you could take a few seconds to leave an honest review or a star rating on Amazon. (A star rating takes just a couple of clicks).

By leaving a review, you'll be helping other parents discover this success skills resource for their middle schoolers.

To leave a review & help spread the word

SCAN
HERE

INTRODUCING
THE LIFE SKILLS FOR
TWEENS

If you enjoyed this book, you'll love our best-selling book "Life Skills for Tweens". Packed with 70+ practical skills and tips to help your tween develop the essential skills and put them into practice.

AVAILABLE ON AMAZON...

Scan the code to buy a copy on Amazon

Made in United States
North Haven, CT
18 August 2023

40436438R00088